The Power

OF

Enneagram

JOHN TURNER

Table of Contents

Introduction 1

Chapter 1

The Enneagram of Personality 5

Chapter 2

Type One: The reformer/perfectionist 12

Chapter 3

Type Two: The Helper/Giver 19

Chapter 4

Type Three: The Achiever/Performer 25

Chapter 5

Type Four: The Individualist/Performer 31

Chapter 6

Type Five: The Investigator/Observer 38

Chapter 7

Type Six: The Loyalist/Skeptic 44

Chapter 8

Type Seven: The Enthusiast/Epicurist 50

Chapter 9

Type Eight: The Challenger/Protector 56

Chapter 10

Type Nine: The Peacemaker/Mediator 62

Chapter 11

The Influence of Wings 68

Chapter 12

Integration and Disintegration Points 73

Chapter 13

Subtypes 78

Chapter 14

Triads 84

Chapter 15

Determine Your Personality Type 90

Chapter 16

The Enneagram and You 96

Conclusion 102

Introduction

Thanks for choosing this book about Enneagram. I'd love to hear your opinion, so make sure to leave a short review on Amazon if you enjoy it. It means a lot to me!

Discover How to Better Understand Yourself and Others, Improving All Relationships". If you are reading this, it is because you are keen on learning more about yourself and those around you. It is highly likely that you have asked yourself on more than one occasion on what it takes to understand the people around you. Moreover, you are more than likely interested in finding a great way to improve your relationships with others in your social circle.

If you have found it difficult to relate to others, or simply want to improve how you communicate with the folks around you, then you have come to the right place. In this book, you will find a collection of thoughts, ideas, tips, and strategies about understanding yourself and those around you.

How is this possible?

With the power of the Enneagram of Personality, you will find a treasure trove of information that will not only help you better understand yourself but also better understand the way humans function in general.

Yes, that's right.

You don't need an advanced psychology degree to gain a good understanding of the way people act, and react, under given circumstances. The Enneagram has made it a lot simpler for the average individual to gain a solid grasp of how the human psyche works based on the various personality types that apply to people.

When you can fully comprehend the way your personality works, you can get a better sense of who you are concerning those you come in contact with regularly. Besides, this understanding of yourself will allow you to position yourself in such a way that you can along with others much more easily.

But that's not the only thing that understanding the Enneagram can do for you. When you understand the Enneagram, you can get a better sense of the way others around see the world and the way they react to the various circumstances they come into contact with. This is a powerful understanding as it allows you to make sense of the way people act and the reason why they do the things they do.

This is powerful stuff indeed.

As such, this book is intended for anyone who is looking to, firstly, gain a better understanding of who they are. Sure, there are plenty of personality tests out there. There is an abundance of information on personality types and so on. But the fact of the matter is that many of these tests are rather limited in their scope.

Then, you have complex personality tests such as the Myers-Biggs which requires training to administer it correctly. While this is no denying that proper examinations such as the Myers-Biggs are certainly valid, the fact remains that they are long, costly and require a considerable investment in terms of time.

Also, this book is intended for the individual who is looking to simply improve their relationships. These relationships can range from average workplace interactions to deeper and more meaningful relationships such as with family, close friends and romantic partners. After all, wouldn't it be great if you could truly understand what's going in someone else's head?

Sure, it is impossible to read minds, at least as far as we're concerned, but truthfully, when you understand the way an individual's personality is structured, you can have a solid lead as to what another person might be thinking.

Furthermore, this book is intended for anyone who is a student of human psychology and behavior. That is why the value that the study of the Enneagram provides is useful to gain a fresh perspective on what may seem like inexplicable reactions and behaviors on the part of those whom you come into contact with.

Now, you might be asking yourself, how can the Enneagram help me understand why others act the way they do?

The effectiveness in the Enneagram lies in the fact that it is a model of the human psyche. This model can create a representation of the human psyche through a series of personality types. Each personality type contains a set of traits that are inherent to that personality type. Thus, an individual of a given personality type will be expected to behave and react in a given manner. This makes human behavior far more predictable than you might have initially thought.

Additionally, your understanding of the Enneagram's personality types will help put your personality into focus. This is the starting point. When you can gain a deeper understanding of who you are and why you act the way you do, you will be able to put yourself into a much broader context. Then, your visualization of the remaining personality types will enable you to detect the behavioral patterns of such personality types in such a way that you will be able to anticipate the way individuals will react.

Of course, there is a great deal of science behind the Enneagram. But the great thing about it is that you don't have to go through a vast amount of work and study to get the most out of it. By reading this book thoroughly, you will be well on your way to unlocking the secrets of the Enneagram. You will be able to make the most of your newfound understanding of the various personality types.

By the end of this book, you will have answered plenty of questions you might have wrestled with previously. These answers will lead you to improved relationships, better opportunities and an improved sense of self.

You will find that this book has been written in a sequential manner that will allow you to go through all of the information about the study of the Enneagram in a digestible manner. It is easy to understand and written in a way which your reading will simply flow.

So, what are we waiting for?

Let's jump right on in.

Chapter 1

The Enneagram of Personality

We will kick things off with this chapter on what the Enneagram of Personality is, what it can be used for, and how you can apply it to your everyday life. It is important to remember that the practical applications of the Enneagram are meant to be within your rea-life, everyday context. We are not talking about some abstract, esoteric science that will leave you with more questions than answers. We are looking to focus on the practical aspects of the Enneagram which will help you get ahead in your pursuits.

The Enneagram of Personality is a model of the human psyche. That is what it boils down to. The Enneagram is intended to systematize the way the human mind works in such a way that seemingly random reactions and behaviors are part of a logical pattern that responds to a specific model that you can identify in every person you meet.

Hence, the Enneagram model is based on nine personality types. Each type has its traits which tend to dominate how an individual behaves. This means that the traits identified in each personality type would be considered as the predominant traits of an individual's personality.

Of course, nothing is black and white in life. There are nuances in every individual which make a clear-cut application of each personality type impossible. This means that every person will have a predominant personality type but will ultimately have traits of other types.

The combination of predominant traits and the influence of secondary traits are what make up the complex apparatus that is the human psyche. The patterns identified in each personality type will enable you to, firstly, gain a broad understanding of the way the psyche of a given person works. Then, the secondary traits observed in a person will shed more light on an individual's overall behavioral patterns.

It is important to note that how you can determine the various personality types is through the administration of a test. These tests consist of questions that can be answered in such a way that you can create a broad profile of an individual's mindset. The great thing about the Enneagram is that you won't have to administer complex tests that require special training to both administer and interpret.

The tests used to determine personality types based on the Enneagram of Personality are very straightforward and contain relevant information for both the test-take and the administrator. Moreover, these tests are simple enough and non-invasive. This is a stark contrast with most psychological evaluations in which test-takers are often bombarded with invasive questions. More often than not, test-takers dodge these questions thus leading to inaccurate results at the end of the examination.

A great place to start with Enneagram testing is https://enneagramtest.net/. In this website, you can find a short, non-invasive test that will reveal your predominant personality type. The test contained in this website can help you, and anyone interested in taking it, gain an introduction into the nine personality types.

A more comprehensive test based on the Riso-Hudson Enneagram Indicator can be found at https://www.9types.com/rheti/index.php. This test is slightly longer than the one found at enneagramtest.net and provides additional insight into the various personality types.

Also, the Enneagram Institute offers a similar type of test. This only difference is that this test is offered through professional evaluation services that have a cost attached to administering the test. Its results are believed to be the standard in terms of the Enneagram of Personality. As such, this could become an interesting option if you are keen on getting a professional assessment based on the Enneagram.

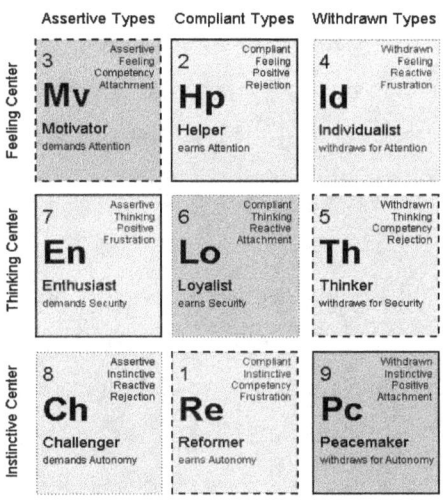

Source: Fitzel.ca

Based on the results obtained through the Enneagram test, one of the nine personality types can be identified for a test taker. Once again, it is worth noting that the main personality is determined based on the predominant traits observed in the individual.

As such, the Enneagram model poses nine personality types from which an individual can derive their main traits. Let's take a look at what these nine personality types are:

1. The reformer/perfectionist
2. The helper/giver
3. The individualistic/performer
4. The achiever/performer
5. The investigator/observer
6. The loyalist/skeptic
7. The enthusiast/epicurist
8. The challenger/protector
9. The peacemaker/mediator

As you can see, each personality type is identified by a name made up of two general descriptors. This is intended to give you an idea of what the personality type is just by looking at the name. Naturally, there is far more to it than that. Nevertheless, it is possible to derive meaning from each one just by taking a cursory glance.

Naturally, when you delve deeper into each one of these items, the components that make up every one of these personality types reveals a profound level of understanding about how an individual will act, and react, in their day to day interactions with the world.

So, let's take a general overview of each of the personality types. We will be presenting a very concise description of each one.

Naturally, we will be taking an extensive look into each one in individual chapters.

- The reformer/perfectionist is the rational and idealistic kind. Type one is principled, purposeful, self-controlled, and perfectionistic.
- The helper/giver is the caring and interpersonal type. Type two is demonstrative, generous, people-pleasing, and possessive.
- The individualistic/performer is the success-oriented and pragmatic type. Type three is adaptive, excelling, driven, and image-conscious.
- The achiever/performer is a sensitive and withdrawn type. Type four is expressive, dramatic, self-absorbed, and temperamental.
- The investigator/observer is an intense and cerebral type. Type five is perceptive, innovative, secretive, and isolated.
- The loyalist/skeptic is the committed and security-oriented type. Type six is engaging, responsible, anxious, and suspicious.
- The enthusiast/epicurist is the busy and fun-loving type. Type seven is spontaneous, versatile, distractible, and scattered.
- The challenger/protector is a powerful and dominating type. Type eight is self-confident, decisive, willful, and confrontational.
- The peacemaker/mediator is the easygoing and self-effacing type. Type nine is receptive, reassuring, agreeable, and complacent.

As you can see, the main descriptors for each personality type are very straightforward. If you would like to make a quick assessment of your personality type, read through each one of the types and choose the one that you feel best describes you. Based on this, you can get your first taste of the way the Enneagram of Personality works in real-life action.

The great thing about the Enneagram of Personality is that you can use these personality types to better position yourself within the social circle that finds yourself in. For example, companies use personality types to gain a better understanding of the people working in a single department. This is especially useful when team members aren't getting along.

As such, companies are willing to invest the time and money that it takes to implement the knowledge derived from the Enneagram. Also, companies administer the Enneagram test to know their candidates better during recruitment. Now, it should be noted that this isn't a question of using this test to filter out candidates. The main point of using this test is to see how a particular individual would fit into the organization.

Consequently, the Enneagram can be utilized to place individuals where they would best fit with the existing team members. In many ways, it's like being able to fit the parts of a machine to exact specifications.

Beyond recruitment, companies also use this test to repair broken-down relationships. This is especially true when departments or entire companies have trouble getting along. Often, companies have significant events, such as a merger or acquisition, in which relationships tend to deteriorate. In such cases, this test can help team members gain a better understanding of each other's behavioral patterns. What this does is highlight the fact that many of the reactions that people have are not a reflection of personal problems. Rather, they are just the effect of how an individual reacts to the circumstances surrounding them.

On a more personal level, the Enneagram is a great way of figuring family dynamics. For instance, some parents are having a hard time understanding their kids. Some families are having trouble relating to one another. Hence, the Enneagram is a way in which individuals can gain a deeper insight into themselves and their relatives. And just like the workplace, this enables folks to repair relationships and find the best way to communicate.

As you can see, the Enneagram is certainly a valuable tool when it comes to self-development and self-exploration. By understanding what makes you tick on a deeper level, you will be able to fully embrace who you are and why you do the things you do. When you reach that point, it is like playing the game of life in hack mode.

Chapter 2

Type One: The reformer/perfectionist

In this chapter, we are going to be diving in headfirst into the Type One personality which is known as the "Reformer" or the "Perfectionist". You will find most references to this type as the "Reformer" though you will also find some references as "perfectionist".

With this first type, there is a duality between change and perfection. As the name suggests, the Reformer is all about seeking change. However, it should be noted that this isn't about change for the sake of change. We are talking about change with a purpose.

As such, change with purpose refers specifically to finding constant improvement above all things. This is fueled by a dedicated and methodical work ethic that is hard to beat. Type One as organized, orderly and meticulous about the way they go about doing things. Thus, the perfectionist side of the personality type enables the individual to find the path to achieving improvement.

Type One is also driven by a high sense of morals. In that regard, they are driven by the principles and values they hold dear. This, in turn, becomes a guiding light for them in their quest for what they believe is right and wrong. It is not rare to see Reformers have a strong sense of duty and a clear differentiation of what is right and wrong.

The main fear of Type One is to become corrupted or defective. This has as much to do with compromising their morals as it does with their performance. Hence, a Reformer will find it hard to accept subpar performance. This personal commitment to performance can lead this personality type to put a considerable amount of pressure on themselves.

The main driving force, or desire, for the Reformer, is to be good, to have integrity and attain balance. Of course, this is easier said than done. Nevertheless, Type One strives to make its best effort in achieving what they believe to be fairness and justice.

Perhaps the most important thing to keep in mind with Type One is their intrinsic motivation to be right, to improve things, and to have things move along under the guidance of their principles. On the flip side, Type One doesn't take criticism too kindly. This is important to keep in mind as Reformers try to stay away from criticism that can lead to the judgment which, in turn, can lead to condemning a given attitude or behavior.

Notable Type Ones are Nelson Mandela, Joan of Arc and Michelle Obama among many other luminaries. These notable Types Ones are classic examples of how the Reformer is constantly seeking to bring about change while upholding the most virtuous values. In fact, as the case of Nelson Mandela, this type would rather endure prison than give up their beliefs. Joan of Arc lost her life over her beliefs. Michelle Obama brought about a revolution with grace and poise worth of a First Lady.

Considering how the Reformer is all about change, these individuals have made it their life's mission to change the world around, but not to suit their own, personal needs. Rather, they intend to change their surroundings in such a way that their values and principles are upheld at all costs.

This leads the Reformer to be incredibly idealistic. Of course, it should be noted that many of these values are culture-specific. For example, Nelson Mandela fought for a very different set of values than Joan of Arc. Granted, they lived centuries apart, and while their circumstances were completely different, their mission was the same: to rid the world of the tyranny they felt was unfairly oppressing their people.

As a result of this personal mission, Type One tends to be very results-oriented. What this means is that a Reformer's mission is guided by some tasks and results that need to be achieved. This could something as simple as organizing their local community to pushing major changes in national legislation.

Such monumental changes have been the result of the personal mission of a Reformer. A great example of this is Mahatma Gandhi. Like Nelson Mandela. Gandhi fought against an oppressive system that was unjustly punishing his people. Yet, the genius in Gandhi's resistance was a non-violent approach. This led to radical changes resulting in a transformational chain of events.

It is important to take into consideration that Reformers tends to be quite the perfectionist. This is due to their results-oriented nature. Since Reformers tend to be very organized and methodical, they will demand that things be done in a certain way as per their specifications. This can become a very negative trait if not properly addressed.

Consequently, one of the biggest challenges that Type One has to face is the fact that they can't control everything no matter how hard they try. This allows room for error. And while a Reformer simply cannot tolerate errors, the reformer needs to accept the fact that not everything can be "perfect".

This is why the "perfectionist" tag added to the name of this personality type is apt. In the worst of cases, the perfectionist personality can lead an individual to become demanding and even overbearing. As a result, the perfectionist needs to understand that they cannot control everything around them. This attitude may also lead to unfair expectations of others as they may hold others up to the same standards, they hold themselves up to.

It is important to note that this rather extreme attitude of the Reformer can develop over time particularly when the individual finds themselves in situations in which they have to overcome large amounts of adversity.

Nevertheless, when considering how Reformers hold themselves accountable for their actions, it is quite common to see these individuals think their actions through. Perfectionists are well aware that their actions have consequences. This is the reason why they tend to overthink the things they do. They feel that if they make a mistake, they may compromise their values, and by extension, their life's mission.

Now, it is also important to consider that the development of the Type One personality is based on levels. Each level indicates the degree of growth that the individual has attained. Thus, level 1 is the level at which the personality type is at its best while level 9 is where the least optimal level of performance can be found.

Types One loves to shoot for level 1. Since they are constantly seeking to improve, they will certainly take achieving level 1 very seriously.

In **level 1**, the Reformer is at their absolute best. At this point, the Reformer can understand that they cannot control everything. Also, they accept a certain degree of mistakes as they also understand how mistakes can be a learning experience as well.

As far as **level 2** goes, the Reformer is humane, polite, kind and helpful, among other things. They tend to be leaders though they may be too analytical and logical at times.

At **level 3**, values, commitment and a strong work ethic are the main driving force behind a Type One. They are focused and determined to achieve their goals.

Levels 1, 2, and 3 are considered to be healthy levels, that is, the level in which a regular person will exhibit their best traits.

In **level 4**, you may find Reformers' feelings dissatisfied or even disenfranchised. This can lead them to take matters into their own hands and become advocates and supporters of specific causes. They may also lead them to do volunteer work in the hope of changing the world for the better.

In **level 5** Reformers tend to be a bit too careful. They will not engage in any activities that are not aligned with their principles. Think of a politician that will or will not do an activity because they feel that it does not reflect their ideals.

In **level 6**, Reformers tend to get very judgmental or extremely picky with the things they do, the people they talk to and their expectations from those around them. At this level, they are very hard on themselves.

Levels 4 through 6 are considered to be "average" levels. But levels 7 through 9 are considered to be "unhealthy" levels as the negative traits of this personality type become more and more predominant.

For **level 7** Reformers, these individuals can become overbearing and patronizing as they feel they are the only ones who hold the truth. They can an incessant need to be right.

In **level 8** Reformers are more judgmental and can become obsessed with perfection. This is where "neat freaks" may emerge. They are also dogmatic in their beliefs.

In **level 9** Reformers are at the most complex level for this personality type. At this point, Reformers can show signs of depression. Also, they can become so obsessive that they can develop obsessive-compulsive disorder.

As you can see, the Reformer type is rather extensive. Also, they may become addicted to, or obsess, with cleanliness and order. Also, they may use alcohol as a coping mechanism for the wrongs they are unable to right.

So, here are some tips to consider for Type One who want to continue improving themselves:

- Relax. Don't take things too seriously. Of course, some situations must be treated very seriously. But in general, just try to relax a bit more.

- Teach. Reformers are usually great teachers. They love to show others how things can be done. Type One is a generally great teacher.
- Watch yourself. It may be very easy to spot the mistakes that others are making. But Type Ones needs to acknowledge that they are not perfect and make mistakes as well.
- Keep your emotions in check. Reformers may become highly emotional especially when they witness injustice or unfair treatment. While standing up and being vocal is important, letting emotion take over may lead to negative consequences.

Finally, it should be pointed out that Type One generally gets along with everyone. At the same time, they tend to grind up against virtually every other type. So, this means that a Type One should try to find a balance between their crusades and circumstances around them. They also need to recognize that we are all human and therefore make mistakes.

In a nutshell, Type One needs to live by their values but without making their will more important than that of others.

Chapter 3

Type Two: The Helper/Giver

In this chapter, we are going to focus on the personality type known as the "Helper". This personality type is also referred to as the "giver". Also, you will see this type referred to as Type Two.

As this type's name would suggest, the Helper is the type of individual who is focused on helping those around them regardless of the circumstances. They are the kind of person who is focused on making sure that others are happy and comfortable. Needless to say, these are folks who can be found in occupations that are geared toward helping others such as caregivers, paramedics and so on.

When Types Two are at their best, they are often selfless and altruistic. They are capable of exhibiting unconditional love. Most importantly, they are always focused on helping those in need. Under this type, you can picture humanitarian aid workers or folks who volunteer for charitable causes.

Some luminaries under the Types Two category include Pope John XXIII, Eleanor Roosevelt, and Bishop Desmond Tutu. These notable figures illustrate a penchant for humanitarian work, such as Eleanor Roosevelt, while exuding peace and compassion as seen in Pope John XXIII and Bishop Tutu.

By most standards, Types Two individuals are those who are first to offer help in times of need. There is no need to ask Types Two to volunteer. They are always ready, willing and able to give their time, effort and talents to causes they truly believe in.

Perhaps this is an underlying issue that needs to be considered. When Types Two truly believe in a cause, or if they see that a person genuinely needs help, they are willing to spring into action at a moment's notice. However, if they feel that the cause does not warrant their efforts, then they may refrain from being the first to enter the fray.

Types Two are the kind of folks who get personally involved in the lives of others... but in a good way. These are not the folks who show up for work every day and see people as numbers. They take a genuine interest in seeing people for what they are: people. A good example of these individuals are those caseworkers who go the extra mile, doctors who will call up patients to see how they are doing, or teachers who take a personal stake in the wellbeing of their students.

When Helpers are balanced and in sync with their life's mission, they are the most generous, loving, caring and compassionate individuals that you will find. Think of those humanitarian aid workers who are living in deplorable conditions, yet they feel fulfilled because they have found their true calling. They won't care about finding themselves in adverse conditions so long as they can help others in need.

However, the flip side of the incredibly loving personality type is an excessive involvement in others' lives. This may lead them to become overly nosy. They may even feel they have a right to tell others how to run their lives as they feel compelled to spare people from themselves. Needless to say, Types Two that finds themselves acting in this manner will cause more harm than good. After all, Types Two may have a hard time understanding the difference between people who need help and people who want to be helped. As such, if a person needs help, but is unwilling to cooperate, may spur a Types Two to become involved despite the other party's reluctance.

One of the biggest concerns for Types Two is a feeling of worthlessness, that is, they may become sad and depressed if they feel they are no use to anyone. This is rooted in the innermost need to be of service. Hence, Types Two biggest desire to serve others regardless of the circumstances. Consequently, their biggest fear is to be unable to serve and thereby become useless to their peers and those around them.

In return for the often, self-sacrificing attitude, Helpers seek some sort of validation. While these individuals offer their efforts without seeking anything in return, they do seek some sort of validation. For instance, they may become distraught if a person whom they wish to help refuses their offer. This lack of validation may lead a giver to feel reject and worthless.

As such, Types Two need to become focused on the fact that they do have a lot to offer to everyone around them. The difference may lie, however, in the way that others may perceive their value. This is where it becomes very difficult for Helpers to acknowledge the fact that not everyone is seeking their even if they do need it.

Nevertheless, when Types Two are allowed to shine, they will do so in the best possible way they can. You will not hear them complaining even if they are under stress and harsh conditions. They will rise to the occasion every time they are needed.

In terms of each level of development, Helpers will transition through various stages. Here is a breakdown of each level of development for this type.

In **level 1**, Types Two are extremely selfless, humble and will give their unconditional love and support to those who need it. These are family members who will stop at nothing to see their loved ones feel well. These are the employees that truly care about their company or business owners who take a genuine interest in their employees' wellbeing. Also, you will find teachers, doctors, lawyers and so on, who make each person their own, personal business.

In **level 2** Helpers are thoroughly empathetic, kind and supportive. They will be concerned about others' needs and wants. They are dedicated to the wellbeing of those around them. They will not take long to forgive someone for their faults.

At **level 3** Helper is a very positive and upbeat individual who is looking to serve others. They are active in their community. They exude love and care especially with those who need a helping hand. They often volunteer for charitable work.

Levels 1 to 3 are an example of how a Type Two will behave when in a healthy stage of development. The following levels, 4 to 6, reflect the way a Type Two would behave when situated in an average stage of development.

In **level 4**, Helpers are "people pleasers". This is, of course, a double-edged sword as people-pleasers are not always fulfilled in what they do. They often find themselves being stressed out over gaining people's approval and validation. Needless to say, this can grow into a rather complex situation. Nevertheless, folks at this stage are very friendly and helpful individuals.

At **level 5** Helpers can exhibit traits in which they are nosy and intrusive. They tend to meddle in other people's business. While this may not be as evident as in other individuals, they do take things far too personally. These folks feel compelled to tell others what to do.

In **level 6**, Givers begin to feel that they are the most important person in the world. These are the types who feel that a company cannot run without them, a family will crumble if they leave, or the world will stop if they are not around to solve things for others. This stems from a lack of validation in which they feel they are not getting the recognition they feel they deserve.

Next, the unhealthy levels show what a Type Two will act when they find themselves in a lower level of personal development.

In **level 7**, Helpers can become manipulative. They may guilt people into doing things. They may even engage in some type of substance abuse to cope with feeling though food tends to be their preferred coping mechanism.

In **level 8** Givers are bent on getting their way. They can be domineering and resort to coercive measures to get people to do what they want. They feel they ought to get repayment for their efforts and service to others.

Finally, **level 9** Types Two can find a logical explanation for the abuse they inflict on others. A classic example of this is an abusive parent that justifies such behavior on their child under the pretense of "disciplining" them. These individuals may end up suffering from chronic health issues as a result of the somatization of their unvalidated feelings. Their ultimate goal is to burden others to get the attention they seek.

In general terms, Types Two can find a path to growth in the following ways:

- You need to help yourself before you can help others. If you are not well, you will never be able to help others be well.
- Make sure you are clear of why you are helping others. Try to avoid disguising ulterior motives with an apparent selfless intention of serving others.
- It is very important to avoid seeking attention for your good deeds. While validation is important, it is also self-destructive to feel that you need recognition for every good deed you do. Often, the best deeds go unnoticed.
- Also, it is important to recognize others' sincere gratitude and their desire to be helped. A kind "thank you" can be validation enough when you help someone. By the same token, a person who does not wish to be helped needs to be left alone until they seek the help they need.

On the whole. Types Two are some of the most selfless and inspiring people in the world.

Chapter 4

Type Three: The Achiever/Performer

In this chapter, we are going to be taking a look at the "Achiever" personality type. We will also be referring to this personality type as Type Three. Furthermore, this personality type can also be referred to as the Performer type. This should not be confused with one other personality type that also carries the performer label. Nevertheless, they do hold striking similarities though they are completely different personality types.

This personality type, as its name indicates is all about getting results. This is the most pragmatic and success-oriented of the nine types in the Enneagram. These folks are very practical and will find the best and most efficient way to get things done. Period. While they enjoy the finer things in life, they are focused and driven by achieving the goals they have set out to accomplish at the outset of their endeavors.

When they are at their best, Type Threes are excellent executors. They are the kind of people that get things done. They can make the most of the resources they have while minimizing the time and effort it takes to make things happen.

The basic, underlying fear of Type Threes is a sense of worthlessness, that is, not being able to achieve what they set out to do in life thereby not contributing to themselves and their community. Thus, their biggest motivation is a sense of being valuable to themselves and those around them. This is what drives them to achieve as much as they can. Ultimately, they seek the recognition that comes with being the best in their fields or achieving great success, the likes of which, few people can accomplish.

Under this category, some of the most accomplished individuals come to mind. Some great examples are Boxer Muhammed Ali, former President Bill Clinton, Motivational speaker Tony Robbins, and golfer Tiger Woods.

As you can see by the exemplary individuals listed under this personality type, Type Threes are highly focused on getting results. Indeed, a pragmatic results-oriented approach is needed if you are going to be the most powerful person in the world, that is, the President of the United States. In the case of Tony Robbins, you can see how his work is geared toward helping people achieve what they want to get out of their lives. Furthermore, Tiger Woods is an example of how hard work and dedication can help you climb to the top of your respective field. As for Muhammed Ali, he becomes the best in his field despite humble beginnings. He was able to transform talent into success as a result of his efforts.

If you identify yourself under this personality type, then you can appreciate the value of hard work and dedication in achieving the goals that you have set out for yourself. It should be noted that it is not the goals and endeavors themselves that count, rather, it is the dedication and willingness to achieve them that makes the difference.

When Achievers are balanced and healthy, they are valuable members of their community insofar as their contributions help to make changes in their surroundings. These are the individuals who will make community events happen, get school fairs off the ground, or make charitable drives successful. They are very cheerful and upbeat about rolling up their sleeves and getting down to business.

However, the flipside of Type Threes is becoming too focused on outcomes and not on the people surrounding them. For example, they will value material possessions over family and measure success in terms of money rather than happiness. These folks can descend into workaholics who place very little value on their home life. They may also become frustrated when they don't get the results they expect. In their worst moments, they will be quick to dismiss people when they don't get the result they want before actually giving them a chance.

Hence, the balance between results and expectations is important for Achievers. Achievers, who are also performers, need to understand that not everyone is quite as driven as they are. Some folks would rather enjoy the ride regardless of how long it takes them to get there. It should be noted that Type Threes are performers because they are all about doing. Achievers who play team sports are known for being great leaders who push their teammates to achieve their collective goals.

Let's take a look at how Type Threes act and react based on their level of personal development.

Firstly, healthy levels 1 to 3 reflect the following attitudes:

In **level 1**, Achievers are authentic, self-accepting and focused. They are very humble and modest folks who have a great sense of humor. They value teamwork and collective success.

In **level 2** Achievers are highly self-confident and competent people. These are the best bosses you could ever work for as they are focused on helping others become the best they can be. They are creative in finding solutions to common obstacles to getting results.

For **level 3,** Achievers' ambition is a great driving force, that is, positive ambition. This ambition is manifested in their desire to achieve change, reach their goals and be the best they could be. These individuals are highly admired for the results they can get in their chosen field.

Now, let's take a look at average levels of development, that is, levels 4 to 6.

Level 4 Achievers are highly competent individuals. These are very efficient employees who are driven to reach their personal and corporate goals. However, the underlying driving forces in level 4 Achievers is more a fear of failure rather than a desire to achieve.

In **level 5**, Achievers are more concerned about the way they are perceived by others as opposed to doing things out of their desire. As such, their wish to be successful is based more on their social status rather than doing what they wish to do for themselves. These are typical social climbers.

For a **level 6** Achiever, their drive is to impress others. These are folks who look to keep up with the Joneses as opposed to doing the things they want to do for themselves and their families. If they are unable to succeed in impressing others, they will become increasingly desperate to portray themselves as successful.

Let's take a look at the unhealthy levels, that is, levels 7 to 9.

In **level 7**, Achievers are driven by their fear of failure. They are overly concerned about losing facing and being seen as worthless. So, they may resort to exploitation and manipulation to get their way.

Level 8 Achievers can become devious, deceptive and malicious to get their way. They will stop at nothing to achieve what they believe are to be their goals.

For **level 9** Achievers, vengeance becomes their main drive. They will strive to get back at those people whom they blame for their failures. If they believe their parents are at fault for their failures, they will do everything they can to punish their parents for keeping them from achieving their goals.

The biggest potential addiction for Type Threes is workaholism. They may also resort to abuse of stimulants to help them keep up with their pace. They may also become overly concerned with their outward image as beauty may become very important to them.

Here are some recommendations for Type Threes in their development journey.

- It is important to keep true to yourself. You need to be in touch with your feelings so that you understand what is driving you. When you understand what is driving you, you will be able to make sense of the negative feelings that may be spurring you on.
- Fostering positive relationships is important. If you are focused on helping others grow alongside you, you will become a positive influence on everyone around you.
- Focusing on goals and projects which will benefit you and your community is essential. Type Threes can fall into a trap

in which they take on too much. They have a hard time saying "no". So, it is important to keep this in mind.

- Being generous with your time and efforts is a great way of finding balance. So, if you are keen on achieving what you want, but also helping others achieve their own goals, you will be able to balance your feelings of personal development and the sense of worth in the greater community.

Type threes make great leaders. At their best, they can be influential folks who motivate others to be the best they can become.

Chapter 5

Type Four: The Individualist/Performer

In this chapter, we are going to be taking a look at the personality type corresponding to the Individualist or Performer. We will also be referring to this personality type as Type Four as per the order we are following.

The Individualist can be perceived as a negative trait on the surface. This stems from the fact that the Individualist is more apt to be introspective, that is, more in tune with themselves rather than being more outward and expressive. One might consider that the Individualist is the opposite of the Helper in the sense that the Helper is focused solely on others whereas the Individualist is more inclined toward focusing on themselves.

This is an important distinction to take into consideration as most folks may misinterpret the individualist's nature as being self-absorbed. And while this is true in the lower levels of development, the fact of the matter is that the Individualist is capable of great sensitivity and care so long as they are provided the opportunity to act on their own without pressure from external sources.

It is also worth mentioning that this personality type is very keen on self-development and improvement. However, this individual is more inclined to their personal development as opposed to the Reformer who is more inclined in making changes across the board. This is what gives the Individualist a great deal of sensitivity and appreciation for the finer points in life. They are very appreciative of the minutiae in life which tends to go unnoticed by most folks.

The most significant fear for Type Fours is having a lack of self-identity. As such, Type Fours are the kind of folks who are constantly looking to find themselves. These are individuals who are prone to do soul-searching regularly. When they can conquer these fears, they can come to grips with who they are and what they stand for. When they can find their self-identity, they become exceptional in whatever their choose field is.

Hence, Type Fours' biggest wish is to find out who they are. Don't be surprised if you know individuals who spend most of their early adult years traveling the world, or bouncing around from job to job until they finally settle into one chosen profession. Superficially, many folks will accuse them of lacking discipline and focus. However, on a deeper level, all they are doing is looking to find what they wish to achieve out of life.

The biggest driving force behind Individualists is their desire to express themselves, that is, their creativity and individuality. This is what makes them great artists and performers. That is why the second word used to describe this personality type is "performer". Please bear in mind that these are folks who thrive in artistic fields, or sports, in which individual performance is the key. They may not excel in team sports unless they have the opportunity to stand out individually. For example, team sports such as Rugby in which one individual cannot dictate the pace of the game may not be the most suited for this personality type. However, sports such as basketball, in which one individual can be the difference-maker, can be good options for this personality type.

Also, artistic fields in which they are left to their own devices can suit Type Fours very well. While they may thrive in more collaborative efforts, they will be at their best when they can express themselves to the fullest. When you think of Type Fours, think of folks such as Criss Angel, Bob Dylan, Frida Kahlo, and Tennessee Williams. These are artists and performers who have stood out based on their merits. Their legacy is based on their talents as opposed to more collaborative efforts.

A balanced Type Four will accept every facet of themselves. They will embrace the good with the bad. They will accept their virtues as well as their flaws. As such, they won't be intimidated by having to deal with situations and circumstances outside of their comfort zone so long as they feel they can learn something about themselves.

Individualists on the lower end of the self-development scale may become withdrawn and unavailable to most folks. They have trouble socializing and developing meaningful relationships. Often, they may have trouble finding romantic partners and keeping a healthy social life. In extreme cases, some individuals become hermits and close themselves off to the world around them.

It should be noted that Individualists don't seek to be alone. Rather, they place a high value on meaningful relationships. Hence, they are very picky when it comes to the people with whom they socialize. Therefore, if a person does not meet their standards, they will generally refrain from engaging people that won't contribute to their development and growth. One telltale sign of this personality type is a person who says they would rather spend one on one time with a close friend rather than going to a loud party filled with people.

Now, let's take a look at the various levels of development for Type Fours. First, let's look at levels 1 to 3 which are considered to be the healthy levels.

In **level 1**, Individualists are deeply creative and inspired. They value their self-image and seek to portray that outward as an expression of their creativity. They are sensitive individuals who value people and relationships greatly.

Level 2 Individualists are very introspective and find themselves on a continuous search for themselves. They are keen to express themselves through the various artistic means available to them.

A **level 3** Individualist is true to themselves. You may find them living up to code, or standard, that is a reflection of their individuality. They can be shy or withdrawn at times though they have no trouble communicating with others. They can be very kind and helpful so long as they are not overburdened by interactions with others.

The next levels, 4 to 6 refer to average levels of development for the Type Four personality.

A **level 4** Individualist will come off as artistic and creative. They embrace the beauty of life. However, they may live in a fantasy world and become prone to daydreaming more than usual.

In **level 5**, an Individualist will be very much in tune with their feelings and creative nature. Nevertheless, their shy and withdrawn personality may come more into focus. They will be less inclined to partake in social activities shying away from interactions with other folks. While these are hardly socially challenged individuals, they may not be as sociable as the folks in the higher levels of development. As such, they may exhibit signs of withdrawal and unavailability.

Level 6 Individualists will show themselves to be very different from "regular" folks. They may sink themselves into overly melancholic dreams. They may even become detached from the real world to live in a dreamland that they have created for themselves. While these folks are hardly schizophrenic, they tend to lose touch with reality. This leads them to become self-indulgent and often unproductive.

Now, let's take a look at the lower, or unhealthy, levels for Individualists.

In **level 7**, an Individualist may become angry and alienated from the real world. They may claim that no one "gets them". This can be used to justify their lack of social skills and interaction with others. This can lead to feelings of shame and cause withdrawal.

Level 8 Individualists live in torment. They often blame others for their failure to make anything of themselves. They tend to harbor feelings of self-contempt and self-loathing. They may even have thoughts of harming themselves.

Finally, **a level 9** Individualist may end up engaging in self-destructive behavior such as excessive drinking and substance abuse. They will consume anything to help them escape the reality which they face to embrace an alternate reality they wish to create for themselves. These individuals are narcissistic and may even attempt to take their own life.

The biggest plight of this personality type is self-indulgence. This can be seen in a lack of self-control and abuse of food, alcohol, and drugs. They may show signs of narcissism and excessive concern for outer appearance.

Here are some useful tips to get over some of the tougher aspects Type Fours may have to face.

- Monitor your feelings in such a way that you do not allow them to ruin your life. Of course, it is important to worry about the way others perceive you. However, it is important to make sure that this doesn't ruin your life. You are far more than your outward appearance conveys.

- Finding your mission, or purpose, in life will give you a sense of belonging. This will help you to stay productive and contribute to society in a meaningful way.

- To keep your self- esteem and self-confidence running high, try to make the most of every opportunity you have to experience positive results. When you can take positive experiences and build on them, you will be able to make the most of life's opportunities.

- Self-discipline is important. You can build your self-discipline through consistent routines such as regular bedtime and exercise regimen.

- Try your best to put your imagination and creativity to the service of others. For example, you can contribute your artistic talents for the enjoyment of others in addition to your remunerated endeavors. Make a point of providing joy to others through your talents.

Type Fours are certainly the most creative bunch in this entire list of personality types. At their best, they can stand out as some of the most inspiring individuals you will ever meet.

Chapter 6

Type Five: The Investigator/Observer

In this chapter, we are going to be taking a closer look at the Investigator personality type. This is also known as the "Observer". We will also be referring to this personality type as Type Five throughout this chapter.

The Investigator is a highly intellectual personality type that is focused on rationalizing things. The more they can make sense about the things inside them and around them, the easier it is for them to get along with the world.

At their best, Type Fives are very capable individuals who can find answers to some of the most complex issues. If you happen to know a healthy Type Five, they will thrive on the challenge of finding answers to issues that perhaps no one else has been able to find. They are very curious, inquisitive and cerebral.

The biggest downside to the Investigator personality type is that they may become detached of their feelings in favor of a rational approach. As such, they may lack the ability to connect with other folks on a deeper, more emotional level. They may even become emotionally unavailable when they are unable to find answers or make sense of things.

The main driving force pushing Type Fives is their desire to be seen as capable and competent. These are the folks that place a high degree of value on college degrees, honors and academic recognition. In the professional world, they may place a great deal of value on awards. For instance, sports stars will measure their overall value on being champions and getting awards. Often, Investigators in athletics can advance the science of a sport.

The underlying fear of Type Fives is being seen as unintelligent or incompetent. An Investigator may fall into a deep depression if they are unable to succeed in academics or if they get stumped in solving an issue. They may also become obsessed with find the answer to a problem until they find the solution to it.

Some of the most notable Investigator types are: professor Stephen Hawking, pianist Glenn Gould, Microsoft founder Bill Gates and film director Alfred Hitchcock. These folks are luminaries in their respective fields. While they all come from different backgrounds, they all challenged the limits of their chosen fields. They were able to make breakthroughs or achieve outcomes which many had thought impossible to achieve. In particular, Stephen Hawking was considered to be the most intelligent person during his lifetime.

Type Fives are known as Investigators due to their inquisitive nature. They take learning very seriously. To them, the main purpose in life is to be on a constant path to learning. This is something highly positive as it allows for greater introspection. This can lead Type Fives to learn so much about themselves. This is why they are often seen as very mature individuals.

Investigators are also known for their penchant for reflection and daydreaming. Of course, this nature is what enables them to come up with breakthroughs that many of them achieve. Even if their innovations are related to their personal life, they can make dreams happen.

On the flipside, this dreamy nature can lead them to lose touch with reality. When this happens, they may not fully appreciate the world around them. In the worst of cases, their inability to find answers to the questions that take up their attention may lead to frustration, and even depression, since they are unable to figure out why things are the way they are. Therefore, acceptance is one of the biggest challenges for Type Fives.

Perhaps on the biggest strengths of the Investigator personality type is that they don't depend on social validation. They don't need to be told they are smart and competent; they already know it. However, insecurity may take hold of them at some point. When this happens, they may seek validation in terms of awards and recognition. If this validation does not come, they may descend into an anxious state.

Let's take a deeper look at the Investigator type by their levels of personal development.

Levels 1 to 3 correspond to the levels of healthy development.

In **level 1**, the Investigator type is at its best. They are visionary and gain a profound comprehension of the way the world works. They can make the most of the situations around them. They are open-minded and deeply embrace change. They are true pioneers in their respective fields.

Level 2 Investigators are highly perceptive. Their deliver insights that ordinary individuals may not be able to provide. They are constantly searching for knowledge often finding value in their original contributions. They may also be considered quirky at times.

For a **level 3** Investigator, they are prone to achieve full mastery of their chosen field or craft. They can become experts in their respective areas of expertise. The produce original contributions which further the betterment of their communities, and why not, the world.

Next, we will see the average levels of development for Type Fives.

In **fourth level** of development, Type Fives will often find themselves working things out well in advanced before actually engaging in any kind of activity. They need to think things through before they commit to their actions. As such, they tend to overthink things.

In **level 5**, Investigators may begin to detach themselves from the world around them in favor of imaginary worlds. This is generally a response to their dissatisfaction with their reality. Instead of facing a reality that may not be what they expected, they fabricate imaginary circumstances. This may lead them to be perceived as delusional.

A **level 6** Investigator may take on an antagonistic posture against everything that does not mesh with their view of the world. Under these circumstances, Investigators may feel compelled to rebel against the system though not for the sake of positive change but for the sake of being right.

Levels 7 to 9 are considered unhealthy levels for Type Fives. They may exhibit some of the following traits.

In **level 7**, Investigators become isolated and nihilistic. Their detachment from reality becomes even more apparent. They are aggressive and will generally reject anything that they feel does not correlate to their visions of the world. They do not get along well in social settings.

Level 8 Investigators are obsessed with imposing their ideas on the world. They may even begin to show signs of delusional and paranoid behavior. While they are not at a point of mental illness, they are firmly detached from reality. They may become reclusive and completely isolated from the world around them.

Level 9 Investigators may have full-blown mental illness, dementia and even engage in self-destructive behavior. These individuals may seek to take revenge on the world and cause great harm. They would rather destroy the world rather than conform to societal expectations that don't adhere to their perceived version of the world. They would rather take their own lives as opposed to accepting their lack of worth in society.

Those Observers who succumb to addictions may find themselves neglecting their wellbeing such as hygiene, exercise and a balanced diet. They might make use of recreational drugs a habit as means of escaping reality. Otherwise, alcoholism may become an alternative escape.

Here are some tips and ideas which can help Type Fives navigate the waters of the world around them.

- It is important to recognize when you are overthinking things. Sometimes, a healthy balance between reason and intuition can help you make sense of the world. Also, recognizing your unique talents will help you identify your value to society.
- It is also important to take the time to relax and make the most of enjoying life. Being too intense and high-strung for

prolonged periods can lead to physical and emotional burnout.

- Also, try to avoid becoming judgmental. It is easy to denounce anything that doesn't conform with your views of the world. Hence, tolerance is an essential part of being balanced and healthy.

- Furthermore, try to address trust issues that you may develop as a result of being "disappointed" by others. When you feel that others don't follow in your lead, you may feel withdrawn and misunderstood. While there is nothing wrong with feeling out of place at times, there are circumstances in which you may need to be more flexible and tolerant with the situation around you.

Investigators are true visionaries. If you identify with this personality type, then take the time to make your dreams a reality. Find the best way to make you dreams come true.

Chapter 7

Type Six: The Loyalist/Skeptic

In this chapter, we are going to be taking a deeper look at the Loyalist personality type. This type is also referred to as the Skeptic. Furthermore, we are going to refer to this type as Type Six, therefore, the course of this chapter.

The Loyalist personality type can be seen at the "rock". These are highly dependable individuals in which you can count on at all times. That is why reliability is their strong suit. They are committed and disciplined in such a way that they see things through from beginning to end. When you identify with this personality type, you are not the kind that starts off a million things and doesn't see anything through to the end. It is quite the opposite. You are committed to seeing things as the last consequence.

In general terms, Type Sixes are great people to have around. You know they won't flake out on you at the last minute. When they give you their word, you can take that to the bank. However, they do tend to become indecisive when they are not at their best. They also tend to become defensive and evasive when they are not feeling comfortable in a situation. The worst thing that can happen to a Loyalist is to be backed into a corner. If this should happen, they may act out in a rebellious and defiant manner.

The most important driving force behind Type Sixes is security, stability, and support. They seek to have a stable environment at all times. If they lack a stable foundation, they will become overly anxious. This can lead them to feel unprotected. Hence, their biggest fear is to feel adrift, that is, floating through life without a sense of direction.

It should also be noted that the Loyalist type has no problem with following orders. They will recognize their place in the chain of command and roll with the punches. However, they will lash out if the official leadership does not provide the guidelines they are supposed to provide. While Loyalists have no trouble taking charge, they need to have guidelines and direction as much as possible.

Some notable Type Sixes include actor Robert DeNiro, former President Richard Nixon, film director Michael Moore, and philosopher Krishnamurti.

These notable figures all encompass the Loyalist nature, that is, they provide stability to those around them. In particular, former President Richard Nixon presided over one of the most difficult periods of American history. And while he stands as the only US President to have resigned, he is remembered for having taken some of the most difficult decisions in history.

The folks who are identified as a Type Six receive the moniker as the "Loyalist" for good reason. In addition to being the most dependable type in the Enneagram of Personality, these folks are the most loyal to their friends, family, and beliefs. These individuals are the last to turn their back on what they believe in and the people they love. As such, they are incredibly reliable even in the harshest of circumstances.

However, as much as they can serve as the rock of their social group, they also need to know that they have the support of those around them. If you have close to a Type Six, then you need to serve them as a source of support from which they can draw strength. Despite the resolve, Type Sixes are not lone wolves. So, they need to know that someone has got their back as much as they've got others' backs.

Given the fact that the underlying fear of the Loyalist is finding themselves with a lack of support, they may end up lacking self-confidence. This will lead them to doubt their own ability to guide and lead the way. Now, this is not to say that they are not good leaders, but if left alone, self-doubt can creep in and undermine their confidence in their ideas and decisions. This is why they are also known as "skeptics" since self-doubt is an issue Type Sixes must deal with throughout their lives.

When perfectly balanced and healthy, Loyalists will have rock-solid faith in their ideas and decisions. At their worst, they might be unable to function without being led. Thus, they will need constant guidance and support. They may doubt their abilities to a point where they might not be able to fully function independently.

Now, let's take a look at the various personal development levels for the Type Six personality type.

First off, levels 1 to 3 are balanced and health levels.

In **level 1**, the Loyalist type is perfectly independent, self-reliant and able to take charge when needed. They are cooperative and highly dependable. They can become cornerstones of any group, team or institution. They make great leaders and hold to their relationships and convictions.

For **level 2** Loyalists, trust is the foundation of their relationships. They can bond with others, foster cooperative relationships and make solid partnerships. They can elicit the best possible performance from others around them.

Level 3 Loyalists are dedicated to their communities, companies, and families. They are responsible, hardworking and trustworthy. People around them value the stability they bring to the table. They make excellent managers and captains.

Now, let's look at the average levels of development, that is, levels 4 to 6.

In **level 4**, the Loyalist type is reliable and trustworthy. They are good at following authority and can be relied upon to the job done when needed. They need structure and guidance to flourish.

For a **level 5** Loyalist, self-doubt may creep in. They may become anxious and evasive as they try to avoid taking on greater responsibility. They may be prone to procrastination and ambivalence. They need a strong support network to fully realize their potential.

A **level 6** Loyalist may be rather insecure. They may choose to act out and rebel as a means of coping with their insecurities. They may also seek to blame others for their lack of security. If put into a leadership role, they may prove to be authoritarian while showing signs of suspicion, paranoia, and insecurity at a deep level.

Levels 7 to 9 are considered the unhealthy levels for a Type Sixes.

In **level 7**, a Type Six might live in constant fear of having their insecurities exposed. They may easily panic and show their signs of inferiority. They might end up feeling defenseless and may depend considerably on those around them.

Level 8 Loyalists may have feelings of persecution, that is, that someone is out to get them. They may resort to violent behavior to assert themselves in their social circle.

For a **level 9** Loyalist, hysteria may take over. They may have to resort to alcoholism, drug abuse of any other type of substance abuse to cope with their fears and insecurities. These individuals may be unable to fully function in the real world. They may become co-dependent on a parent or spouse. Suicidal tendencies are not out of the questions.

Type Sixes are prone to substance abuse when going through a difficult time. They may also engage in workaholism especially if they become an indispensable member of an organization. They may also resort to caffeine and other stimulants to keep them going through addiction to antidepressants may prove to be evident as well.

Based on the personal development levels, here are some general guidelines which can help Type Sixes fully grow and develop.

- Managing anxiety is key. That is why understanding the root of your anxiety is important to get a grip on it. Please remember that you are not alone. If you feel that there is no one out there for you, then you need to seek help from professionals who can aid you when needed.
- Self-doubt is also a persistent issue. If you feel that you begin to question yourself or the decisions you have made, bear in mind that you have succeeded even more times than you have failed. Your successes are all the evidence you

need to prove that your instincts and judgment are right. It is also important to avoid letting others plant a seed of doubt in your mind.

- Stress management is also an important factor to keep in mind. If you don't get a handle on stress, it can undermine your ability to keep a level head when having to act under duress. Relying on your support network in times of difficulty can become a true lifesaver.

- Thus, developing a strong support network will help you get the grounding you need to keep you from going off course.

Type Sixes are highly dependable individuals who will serve as the cornerstone of a family or organization. If you identify with this personality type, please keep in mind that you don't have to do everything on your own. There are others to support you.

Chapter 8

Type Seven: The Enthusiast/Epicurist

In this chapter, we are going to delve into the personality type known as the "Enthusiast". This type can also be referred to as the "Epicurist". Throughout this chapter, we are going to refer to this type as "Type Seven", as well.

The Enthusiast type in the Enneagram is, by far, the most extroverted and happy-go-lucky type. These are playful, cheerful and simply fun people to be around. They are the life of the party. They are the kind of individuals who can lighten the mood especially if things are tense. Type Sevens should not be confused with "class clowns" since these so-called clowns tend to be folks with low self-esteem that don't mind being the butt of others' jokes.

On the flip side, the Enthusiast type may be considered to be undisciplined and unruly. In the worst of cases, these are individuals who lack direction and purpose. One might consider them to be the opposite of the Loyalist personality type. Nevertheless, they can always be relied upon to crack a joke when most needed.

The fundamental driving force behind the Enthusiast type if they desire to have their needs fulfilled. This may be seen as an entitled nature. In reality, they seek their happiness and pleasure, hence the "Epicurist" tag. They will strive, as much as possible, to have their needs met with the least amount of effort possible. This is why their biggest fear and concern is to deal with pain and deprivation. Thus, they are light on tolerance and steadfastness.

The quintessential Type Seven is actor Jim Carrey. Other notable Type Seven includes legendary composer Mozart, business tycoon Richard Branson, and Academy Award Winner Robin Williams. These individuals all encompass the happy nature of this personality type. Mozart is renowned for having a lighthearted nature despite exploring very serious themes in some of his works. Richard Branson in an ultra-successful businessman who loves to have fun. Robin Williams though is a great example of how much a wonderful and magical person can succumb to the darkest side of this personality type.

In general terms, Type Sevens will light up a room. They are the most lovable and easygoing folks you will ever meet. They are highly sociable and have no trouble making friends, forming strong relationships and getting along well with others in cooperative situations. In the business world, they make great salespeople, public relations agents and some of the most beloved politicians.

On the flip side, their aversion to pain and sacrifice leads most observers to consider them weak and entitled. However, the fact of the matter is that they are not naturally averse to pain and sacrifice. If anything, they will seek to find an easier and better way of doing things. Thus, they will try to avoid grinding along if there is an alternative. For instance, they would much rather drive if they can avoid walking. After all, driving takes less time than walking.

When Type Sevens get the proper support and guidance from those around them, they will have no trouble taking charge and become a positive influence on those around them. When left unsupported, they may resort to a life of pleasures. As such, they may end up "partying" too much or simply avoiding responsibility at all costs.

One common method that Type Sevens engage in is "trial and error", that is, they will seek out various careers, fields of study or disciplines until they find the right one for them. This is often seen as a lack of direction. That is why proper guidance, especially for younger Type Sevens, will help them find their ideal path.

Now, let's take a look at Type Sevens in the various levels of personal development.

Firstly, let's analyze levels 1 to 3, that is, the healthy levels.

In **level 1**, Enthusiasts will have a contagious attitude for life. They are highly positive folks who are awed and inspired by even the simplest things in life. They have a noble spirit that makes everyone happier. They tend to be highly spiritual.

For **level 2** Enthusiast, extroversion is the name of the game. They are very excitable individuals who are lively, cheerful and spontaneous. They light up a room when they enter. They can also be resilient and show great motivation.

Level 3 Enthusiasts are accomplished individuals who rise to the top of their respective fields. They showcase their talents and can often be seen revolutionizing their area of expertise as they search for better ways of doing things.

Let's take a close look at the average levels of personal development, that is, levels 4 to 6.

In **level 4,** the Enthusiast personality type can be seen as a restless individual who is constantly seeking to explore the world around them. They relish in jobs and occupations that won't keep them tied to a desk or an office. They love going out to see the world even if it means taking on more risk than most folks would care for. They are the ones who test the boundaries of the world.

Level 5 Enthusiasts tend to be hyperactive. They just can't seem to settle down. They have a hard time taking "no" for an answer but not always in a good way. They tend to find themselves always doing something even if it is not the most productive thing they could be doing with their time and energy. They may take on too many things at once and end up achieving very little.

A **level 6** Enthusiast will be prone to excess. This may come in the form of excessive greed and materialism. They may become consumed with the idea of looking good, living in luxury and having a lavish lifestyle. They may become pushy and demanding. They will expect others to comfort to their whims.

Levels 7 to 9 correspond to the unhealthy levels for the Enthusiast personality type.

In **level 7,** the Enthusiast may show themselves to be overly anxious. They may also have a hard time controlling their impulses. As such, they may engage in impulse shopping or resorting to addictions to quell their hyperactive nature. Drugs such as marijuana help calm their nerves and anxiety.

Level 8 Enthusiasts are known for mood swings. While they may not be bipolar, they will have erratic changes in mood. This leads to unpredictability which can even offend people. Their impulsive nature can lead to a lack of self-control which can land them in serious trouble.

The **level 9** Enthusiast is at wits end. This individual may have consumed their energy and good spirits. As such, they are completely spent. They may become paranoid, claustrophobic and rely heavily on drugs to keep them going. They may find themselves in deep despair, depression and lash out in self-destructive behavior. Suicide can be a consequence of this level. Bipolar disorder and borderline personality disorder may be issues as well.

In general, Type Sevens struggle with addiction, particularly drug abuse, or any type of stimulant. Also, their hyperactive nature can lead them to burnout. As such, they may become dependent on painkillers and other types of opiates.

Here are some useful tips and strategies which can help Type Sevens stay at their best.

- Self-control is vital. Recognizing when you are feeling impulsive is a great way to find a good balance. If you feel that you are losing control, you can take a step back. That way, you won't act on your impulses leading you to potentially irrational behavior.
- Also, putting others ahead of yourself is a great way in which you can foster strong relationships with those around you.
- Embracing silence and solitude are also great ways of balancing out your social and extroverted nature. Downtime is essential to replenish energy and strength.
- Furthermore, being aware of the quality of your interactions in life will help you to focus on what matters. For example, it is best to have a small group of real friends as opposed to

having a large social circle that is not conducive to meaningful relationships.

- Try to remain focused on what you want out of life. It is easy to bounce around from one place to another. In the long run, however, this unpredictable nature can lead to a lack of direction and structure.

At their best, Type Sevens are wonderful and magical people to be around. They can become the type of person we all aspire to be. That is why honing in on talents and skills can help Type Sevens find the direction they seek.

Chapter 9

Type Eight: The Challenger/Protector

In this chapter, we are going to be taking a look at the eight-personality type of the Enneagram called the "Challenger". This personality type is also referred to as the "Protector". Throughout this chapter, we will be referring to it as Type Eight.

The Protector personality Type is a very strong type by definition. This is the strongest type in the Enneagram as the folks who identify with the personality are geared toward taking care of others. The kind of protection that they provide can be physical, emotional, or perhaps both. They are the quintessential keepers. They are in tune with controlling their environment. As such, they are not afraid of responsibility. These individuals tend to act as heroes and champions.

At its best, the Protector is an individual who will not back down from a fight. They are glorious and often assertive. Their main driving force is to be in control of their destiny. They hate depending on others. They would much rather face incredible odds than lose control.

On the flipside, they can be aggressive and intimidating. They can attack those around them when they don't get their way. They can degrade into bullies. At their worst, they are domineering and egocentric. Needless to say, this is not the noblest side of the Protector.

As a result, the Protector's biggest underlying fear is being hurt and/or losing control. At times, they can be emotionally unavailable as they are afraid of letting others get too close to them. However, this fear can be offset by setting up a system in which they have control of everything that goes on around them. Indeed, the Protector is a control freak.

That is why the main driving force behind the Protector is to be completely independent and self-reliant. They have no trouble working long hours, bearing tough situations or dealing with harsh conditions so long as they have the chance to choose their fate.

Some notable Protectors include humanitarian Oskar Schindler, writer Ernest Hemingway, and United States President Donald Trump. All of these individuals have a steadfast nature in common. They were not afraid to back down from a challenge. Ernest Hemingway worked his way up from being a beat reporter for small-town newspapers to become one of the greatest writers in the history of literature. Oskar Schindler risked his life to save hundreds of Jews from Nazi persecution during World War II. Ultimately, Schindler had to flee to save himself from the Nazis. US President Donald Trump has proven to be steadfast in the face of tremendous opposition from all angles. He is a great example of how the Protector is not afraid of fights to defend what they believe to be right.

It should be noted that the main reference to this personality type is the Challenger since the folks who identify under this description are not afraid of putting up a fight. They will not back down until they have been defeated. And even then, don't be surprised if they come back. After all, what doesn't kill them only makes them stronger.

However, this steadfast nature can quickly degrade into stubbornness. This is important to keep in mind as successful Challengers need to strike a balance between being strong and steadfast while knowing when to back down. As such, there is a fine line between showing no fear and being foolhardy. Often, the Challenger type can take on a fight that is too big for them. Consequently, their defeats can crush their spirit. If such a case were to occur, the Challenger will come back with a chip on their shoulder. Yet, this attitude may lead them to act out of spite and not a sheer desire to help and/or protect others.

While the Protector, or Challenger, is one of the toughest individuals you will meet, they can quickly become overly aggressive, narcissistic and even turn into bullies. If they have a hard time getting a grip on their aggression, they will needlessly run over people who had no intention of harming them. When they are under large amounts of stress, they will lash out against those around them. This makes them very much unlikeable.

Nevertheless, they are pillars of strength from which other individuals can derive fortitude and solace when things are going tough. Challengers are the type of folks whom you can count on to have your back when you get into trouble.

Now, let's take a look at the various levels of development for the Challenger personality type.

The first levels, 1 to 3, pertain to the healthy levels.

In **level 1**, the Challenger type is very disciplined and restrained. They know they have great power and use it to protect others who are not as strong. They use their authority appropriately and courageously stand up for those who need a voice. They know when to back down. They may achieve tremendous exploits of heroism.

Level 2 Protectors are assertive and self-confident. They are, by no means, a pushover. They take initiative and leadership when the situation warrants it. They keep a can-do attitude at all times and will spare no effort to encourage others to get things done.

Level 3 Challengers are decisive, commanding and authoritative without degrading into pushing people around. They take the initiative when needed and raise their voice to champion people and causes that need their support.

Now, let's look at levels 4 to 6, which are considered to be average levels of personal development.

In **level 4**, the Challenger type is prone to self-sufficiency, independence and pragmatism. They don't need anyone to do anything for them. Even when they get into trouble, they don't need help or handouts. Consequently, it may be very hard for them to ask for help when they need it. Their strength may be confused with arrogance and pride.

Level 5 Protectors are control freaks. They need to dominate their environment to ensure that they have control over the situations which may arise. They are proud and often self-centered though not entirely selfish. They are very much interested in imposing their point of view on others.

Level 6 Challengers are feisty. They will challenger everything around them until they get their way. This early manifestation of stubbornness can sabotage their success. They have trouble respecting others' authority. Needless to say, they don't play well with other kids.

Now, let's have a look at the unhealthy levels for the Challenger personality type, that is, levels 7 to 9.

In **level 7**, a Protector may begin to degrade into a bully. They may be ruthless in their actions. They are swift to impart their brand of justice. You are basically with them, or against them. They may descend into a high degree of violence.

Level 8 Challengers may end up developing delusional ideas about their power and authority. They begin to have delusions of grandeur in which they may develop a dictatorial attitude. They believe they are the only ones who hold the right answers. They will spare no effort to get others to go along with them.

In **level 9**, Challengers may well have descended into full dictator mode. They will use violence and force to impose their will. They will not stop until everyone has submitted to their will. They need to be recognized as the supreme leader. These individuals may even be borderline schizophrenics.

Their main addictions lie in self-indulgence. Hence, they may battle with weight their entire lives. Also, they tend to manage high levels of stress. As such, they are prone to diseases such as high blood pressure, stroke and coronary issues. They may also engage in substance abuse.

Here are some key insights to help Protectors develop their abilities to the fullest.

- Self-discipline and restraint are important qualities. You need to recognize your power and how it should be used only to protect others from harm and injustice. Save your energies and focus on times when others need you.

- It is also important to learn how to yield every so often. You don't lose power and authority by admitting that others are right. Taking advice from others only reaffirms your self-confidence as it shows that you are not afraid of listening to others.

- Being self-reliant is a hallmark of this personality type. Yet, don't be afraid to ask for help when you need it. It doesn't make you any less of a champion to recognize that there is something which you cannot do alone. Asking for help will only make others see you as someone flexible as opposed to stubborn.

- Also, try to avoid placing too much emphasis on holding power and control. While it is fundamental for Type Eights to have power and control, do not allow this to cloud your judgment. If anything, delegating authority to others will help you sleep a lot better at night.

When balanced, Type Eights are the ultimate protectors and champions. If you have such a person in your life, you will never vulnerable and unprotected.

Chapter 10

Type Nine: The Peacemaker/Mediator

In this chapter, we are going to be taking a look at the final personality type in the Enneagram. This personality type is the "Peacemaker" which is also known as the "Mediator". Besides, this personality type will be referred to as Type Nine throughout this chapter.

As its name suggests, the Peacemaker is all about finding a happy medium whenever there is the potential for conflict. In many ways, the Peacemaker is the direct opposite of the Challenger. As such, the Peacemaker's goal is to avoid conflict as much as possible. Their main aim is to achieve harmony and togetherness.

Perhaps the biggest misconception is that the Peacemaker is a pushover. That is hardly the case when Type Nines find themselves in balance. A solid and healthy Type Nine will be firm in the posture but will always try their best to find common ground that leads to a win-win for all of those involved.

In general terms, the Peacemaker is easygoing and receptive. At their best, they a very "zen", that is, they hold a great deal of inner peace. As such, they are not at war with themselves. Rather, they know who they are and what they are capable of achieving. This is a feeling of peace that they transmit to their fellows. They are great teammates and colleagues.

When they are not at their best, Type Nines can descend into feelings of loss and desperation. They may feel out of place and shift to the opposite end of the spectrum by becoming jaded and mistrusting of others. Moreover, they may refuse to cooperate with others choosing aloofness and withdrawal.

The innermost element driving Type Nines is their desire for inner peace. Their search for stability and wholeness is what drives them to become who they are. Peacemakers are prone to accepting situations that they may not agree with but will do so out of their necessity for peace. In a way, they fell that if they acquiesce with what others won't, they can put conflict behind them.

On the other hand, a balanced and healthy Type Nine will be able to draw a line in the sand and make their voice heard. They will assert their position as they have no qualms about who they are and what they stand for. This is why a balanced Peacemaker is hardly a pushover.

However, Type Nines' biggest fear is loss. They fear losing their support network or mechanism. They would much rather acquiesce than lose their loved ones and friends. This is why peace is so valuable to them. Peacemakers feel that conflict will ultimately leave them all alone without their support network behind them.

Notable Type Nines include Princess Grace of Monaco, General Colin Powell, former President Ronald Reagan, and ex-Beatle Ringo Starr. An interesting example of these legendary individuals is Ronald Reagan who was at the helm when the Berlin Wall fell. He was instrumental in achieving peace by ending the Cold War, but at no time did he succumb to the pressures of the former Soviet

Union. He was able to stand his ground in defense of democracy around the world.

As mentioned earlier, the Peacemaker personality type is all about peace and harmony. They will also take on the role of mediator whenever possible. This is why the term "Mediator" has been tagged onto this personality type. Type Nines will do whatever they can to help others solve their issues and make the most of the opportunity they have to make peace.

Type Nines also tend to be very spiritual. They are generally in touch with their deeper selves. This is why their desire for peace is so profound. Hence, wholeness takes center stage when going about their life. In some of the more extreme cases, Type Nines may become hopeless romantics and idealists. They may dream of world peace in crisis and war.

On the flipside, Type Nines who lose touch with reality may become too overly optimistic. When reality clashes with their views of a peaceful and harmonious world, they may become jaded and resentful. This is especially true if they feel they have been unjustly wronged. This may, in turn, lead them to feel that they have been cheated.

When Type Nines descend into depression and despair, they may become completely pessimistic and dark. They may even try to numb out their pain through substance abuse or self-harm. In a way, they might feel as though they failed to achieve wholeness. Hence, they take their frustrations out on themselves. Thus, this leads to self-destructive behavior.

Now, let's take a look at the various levels of personal development for the Type Nine personality type.

First, let's have a look at the healthy levels, that is, levels 1 to 3.

In **level 1**, Peacemakers are fulfilled. They are filled with hope and are optimistic to the core. The fight for equality and justice. They will raise their voice for the causes they feel are just. Since they are at one with themselves, they will strive to have deep and meaningful relationships with those they choose to do so.

In **level 2**, Peacemakers are trusting and accepting. They are welcoming especially to those individuals who may have suffered from some type of exclusion of persecution. They are calm, serene and peaceful. The lack malice with themselves. They are simply good-natured people.

Level 3 Peacemakers are optimistic and reassuring. If you happen to have a counselor or therapist of this nature, you will find that they automatically help you feel at ease as soon as you saw them smile. They make great judges as they are impartial and fair, but genuine and caring.

Now, let's take a look at the average levels of personal development, that is, levels 4 to 6.

In **level 4**, a Peacemaker will act more out of fear of conflict that a genuine desire for peace. As such, they will strive to avoid conflict more than solve it. They are very complacent and may have a hard time asserting their position.

For **level 5** Peacemakers, conflict is their prime focus. They try as hard as they can to avoid becoming involved in a conflict. They may begin to withdraw and simply go with the flow. They may even begin to tune out when things begin to get rough.

Level 6 Peacemakers will do everything they can to avoid conflict altogether. They may even begin to shift to the opposite end of the spectrum by becoming increasingly pessimistic and stubborn. They feel that if they can't do anything to solve a conflict, then it's just best to stand by and watch the world burn.

Now, let's have a look at the unhealthy levels for this personality type, that is, levels 7 to 9.

In **level 7**, Peacemakers may feel incapable of dealing with conflict. Any type of issue will cause them to feel. They may even become neglectful of themselves and their duties. They may even start to become out of touch with their feelings.

For a **level 8** Peacemaker, dissociation may become the most effective coping mechanism for conflict. In a sense, they become someone else to get around the issues that bother them. They simply go through the motions when the going gets tough. Fear may get a grip on them.

Finally, a **level 9** Peacemaker may end up becoming a shell of who they once were. They may become completely oblivious to the reality around them. They may become paralyzed by fear and insecurity. They may even crumble completely in the face of adversity. Suicidal tendencies may be something to look out for at this stage.

Here are some tips and strategies which can help Peacemakers find the balance and wholeness they seek:

- Being assertive is fundamental to maintaining harmony. There is a point where you must draw the line to avoid others taking advantage of your agreeable nature.

- It is also important to stay in tune with what is going on around you. If you feel compelled to tune out when things are getting tough, then you might find that circumstances may end up becoming too overwhelming for you to deal with.

- If you find yourself in the middle of conflict, it would be wise to assess your role in the causing or diffusing it. If you find that you are causing the conflict rather than quelling it, then it might be time to take a deeper look at the role you are playing in that situation.

- Also, make sure that stays in tune with your body and your emotions. You need to stay in touch with the way you feel both physically and emotionally.

When at their best, Type Nines can be the comforting folks that you seek to have around you. They can be a soothing presence in the middle of turmoil.

Chapter 11

The Influence of Wings

In this chapter, we are going to be looking at "wings" and how they influence the core personality types of the Enneagram.

In the previous chapters, we took an in-depth look at the core personality types. As we have established, there are 9 core personality types. And while they all have some common elements among them, they are all different personality types.

However, it should be noted that there is no single person who is a pure core personality. What that means is that everyone has influences from other personality types. So, when reading the personality descriptors, if you felt that the descriptions from other personality types applied to you, then you might be getting close to figuring out your wings.

A good comparison of this is the Zodiac. Each Zodiac sign has pure characteristics attached to it. Nevertheless, no one is a pure Zodiac sign. They always influence a secondary sign. This secondary sign is what gives each individual their nuances when it comes to their personality and character.

As such, the same concept applies here. The core personality type that every one of us identifies with is influenced by its corresponding wing. As a result, it is important to understand what that wing is and how that applies to how our personality takes shape.

It should also be mentioned that our environment plays a key role in our overall behavior and personality. Since humans are in constant evolution, there is no denying that the circumstances in which we live in play a vital role in molding the way we handle ourselves. Nevertheless, our core personality remains the same throughout our lifetime.

Here is a good look at how the entire Enneagram of Personality is represented as a whole:

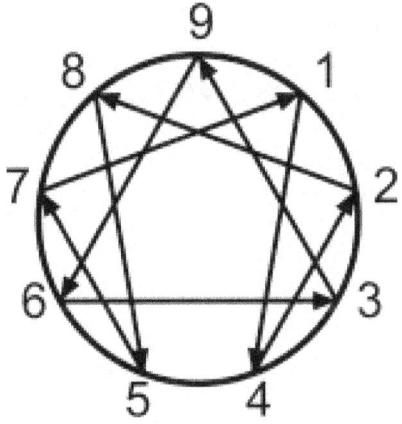

Source: Fitzel.ca

The diagram represents all 9 personality types in action. As you can see, they are all interrelated. Thus, they do not exist in isolation. Quite the opposite, they are all interconnected in one fashion or another. That is why there is a specific order to how we presented the personality types at the beginning of this book.

Once you have identified your core personality type, you can then look at the secondary characteristics which apply to you, that is, your wings. For instance, if you identify yourself as a Type One, then your wings will be Type Nine and Type Two. As such, the personality types adjacent to yours, to the left and the right, are your wings.

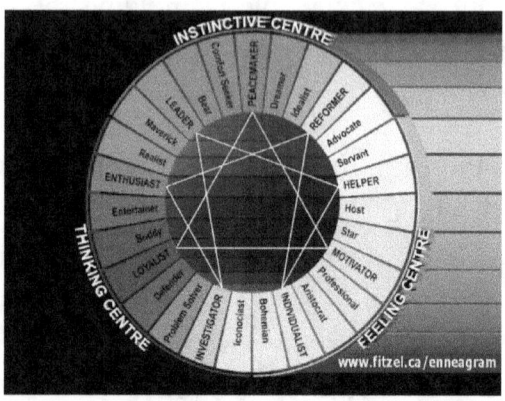

Thus, your wings represent a secondary influence on your core personality. Of course, it should be pointed out that there are no personality types that are better than others. They all have equally positive and negative traits. Consequently, your wings will not "improve" or "affect" your core personality. They are simply additional influences which you must take into account.

In general terms, it is believed that we can only influence one wing. Much like the Zodiac, there can only be one secondary core personality. However, some students of the Enneagram believe that it is possible to influence both wings. For this book, we will entertain the possibility of influencing both wings as experience has shown that both wings can play an influential role in shaping an individual's overall personality.

It is also important to consider that even if there is the influence of two wings, there will always be one "dominant" wing. In that regard, your Enneagram personality test will reveal which of the wings is more predominant.

As such, when you are looking into your core personality, it pays to read up on both wings, the one to the left and the one to the right, to see which of the characteristic may apply most to you. That is why it is a good idea to read up on all nine personality types. That way, you can get a good idea of how these influences may work out on you.

In some cases, some folks have stated that their second wing has developed over time. So, in their younger years, they had their core personality plus their predominant wing. But over time, these folks have indicated that the characteristics of their second wing have evolved. As a result, they feel a greater influence from their second wing. This is why we believe that there is the possibility of influence from the second wing though it is worth pointing out that the development of a second wing may be more the result of experience and maturity rather than an individual's inherent traits.

One other important aspect to consider is the fact that the core personality type and the wings of an individual may be to blend over time. Hence, older individuals may not exhibit the pure traits of their core personality, but rather, a morphed version of their core personality and its wings. Indeed, this is very much possible especially if the individual has been working hard to offset the more negative aspects of their core personality and hone in on the positive aspects of their core personality in addition to those of their wings.

At the end of the day, it is worth mentioning that this can be a conscious effort. What that implies is that you, as a conscious being, can work on and focus on the aspects of your personality which you wish to develop. By the same token, you can choose to let the more negative aspects take hold of you. Of course, there are times when folks need help. In such cases, professional help will certainly aid in getting an individual through a rough patch. Nevertheless, we can all make a concerted effort to improve our personality as we see fit.

Ultimately, your wings are just as influence. Your core personality is what defines the basic makeup of your personality and character. So, do take the time to determine your basic core personality type. That is the perfect starting point for your personal development.

Chapter 12

Integration and Disintegration Points

In this chapter, we are going to be taking a look at a very important part of the transition through the evolution, or perhaps devolution of an individual. As such, the integration and disintegration points provide an important map for reaching one's full potential.

In each of the descriptions for the nine core personalities, we laid out the progression through the various levels of personal development that a person can go through as they make their way across their life.

As such, it is important to understand what each level of personal development is in greater detail.

First of all, we indicated how there are "healthy", "average", and "unhealthy" levels for each core personality type. Each level corresponds to a progression in which the individual may be improving upon themselves thereby unlocking their core personality's best traits, or perhaps sinking into a downward spiral in which their core personality's negative traits come to the forefront.

Thus, it is important to gain a better understanding of how each of these levels can be conceptualized. Here is a breakdown of what each level represents.

Healthy levels:

- Level 1: This is the level associated with "liberation". In other words, the individual has unlocked their potential.
- Level 2: The level is liked to "psychological capacity" meaning that the person has achieved their best mental and spiritual level.
- Level 3: This level is called "social value", that is, this is the level where the individual is contributing the most to their social group and/or community.

Average levels:

- Level 4: In this level, there is an "imbalance of the social role" that the individual is meant to play. There might a lack of awareness regarding the role they are expected to play.
- Level 5: This is also known as the level of "interpersonal control". Hence, this is the level the governs relationships with others around the individual.
- Level 6: This level is referred to as the level of "overcompensation". As such, this level seeks to make up for the things which the individual may be lacking.

Unhealthy levels:

- Level 7: This level is commonly referred to as the level of "violation", this is, there is a breakdown occurring at some point.
- Level 8: This level pertains to "obsession and compulsion". This means that an individual at this level will have succumbed to addictions and fixations on the things they believe they are lacking or that they are missing.

- Level 9: The final level is referred to as the level of "pathological destructiveness". This is the point in which the individual is essentially in self-destruct mode.

Based on the initial assessment carried out to determine a person's core personality, light can be shed on their level of personal development. From there, the individual can determine if they are on a path of integration or a path of disintegration.

To illustrate this path, let's start at the extremes.

Let's suppose that you have taken your assessment and you have found yourself to be at level 1. This means that you are a perfectly integrated and healthy person. While everything may seem great, please bear in mind that there is always the possibility of a trend downward. There are any number of things which can cause you to spiral into a descent: the death of a loved one, the loss of a job, a tragic accident, virtually any major event can trigger a descent into a path of disintegration.

Now, let's go all the way to the other end of the spectrum. Let's consider someone who is deep into level 9 and essentially ready to take their own life. Since there is no further way down, the only way is up. And just like the previous example, there are any number of things that can trigger a reversal on to the path of integration. For example, the discovery of oneself, meeting a wonderfully positive person, or a spiritual awakening, among many other things, can trigger a reversal.

The main thing to keep in mind is that the path to integration, which is generally what we all seek, begins with a heightened sense of awareness. When you are aware of who you are, what you stand for, and your role in life, you can begin to gain a stronger foothold in life.

If you find yourself in the middle of the pack, then you have just as much chance to trend upward as you do downward. What that means is that it is up to you to figure out which way you want to go. The most important action which you can take, today, is to live in the present. The single-most powerful factor that gets people on a downward slope is hanging on the past. Likewise, fearing the future will keep you in a constant state of emotional disarray. Hence, the solution to finding yourself on a path of integration will take you through the present while leaving the past behind. As for the future, you can always deal with that when the time comes.

In general terms, the path to integration, that is growth, will look something like this: 1, 7, 5, 8, 2, 4, 1, 9, 3, 6, 9. What this means we must first move around the entire Enneagram before we can reach the ultimate level of integration. That is why there will be times when you may feel like you're a level 9 before you can reach level 1.

On the other hand, your path to disintegration, or stress, will look something like this: 1, 4, 2, 8, 5, 7, 1, 9, 6, 3, 9. Once again, you will have to bounce around the Enneagram before you can truly fall into the pits of level 9.

It should also be noted that these levels will manifest behaviors according to your core personality and your wings. So, please refer to the descriptions for each personality type so that you can get an idea about the types of feelings you will encounter as you transition through the various levels of the Enneagram.

John Turner

One final note: please bear in mind that you will never have a smooth journey, that is, levels 1, 2, 3, 4 and so on. You first need to experience the various levels of both healthy and unhealthy behaviors before you can truly reach your desired goals for your personal development.

Chapter 13

Subtypes

In this chapter, we are going to be taking a look at what the subtype is in the Enneagram of Personality and how they interact with the various personality types. Also, we will be looking at a more specific understanding of how each of these subtypes can influence your core personality.

The subtypes found in the Enneagram of Personality are essentially related to three main areas that are associated with three essential human needs:

1. The need for self-preservation: this is how we respond to the threat that we perceive.
2. The need for social interaction: these are the networks that we create within our social groups and communities.
3. One on one: these are the personal connections that we make with individuals. This can also be seen as the need for intimacy and finding a mate.

These needs all happen at an instinctual level. What that means is that we are not always fully conscious of when these needs are apparent in us. We tend to fulfill these needs without really paying much attention to them. That is, we don't wake up one day and say, "I need to beef up my self-preservation skills".

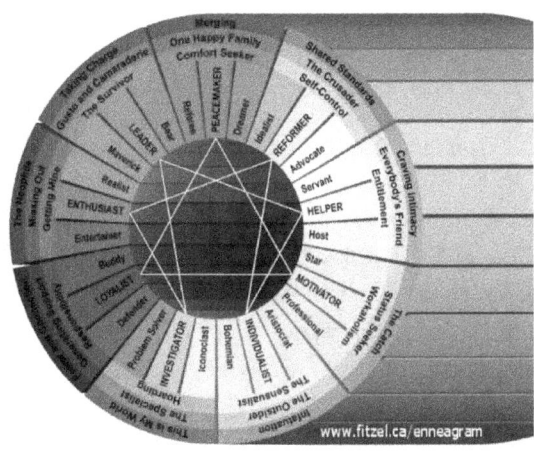

Since these needs are instinctual, they are present in every human being. Consequently, they make up part of our personality. Furthermore, they interact with our core personality type in such a way that it ultimately produces a specific behavioral pattern.

In all, there are 27 subtypes. Now, you might be thinking that's a lot. But it's just a numbers game. In essence, there are 3 instinctual subtypes and 9 core personality types. So, 3 multiplied by 9 equals 27.

With that in mind, let's take a look at how each of the 3 instinctual subtypes plays out with the 9 core personality types.

Instinctual Subtypes		
Self-preservation	Social	One on one
This subtype pertains to survival, which is physical security, shelter, food, and any resources needed to	This subtype pertains to the need for belonging and participation in broader social	This subtype deals with personal and intimate relationships, mating and the need for procreation. It

ensure personal survival and that of the family unit.	circles and communities.	can also extend to close friendships.
Type 1: this type is very much concerned about having order when it comes to all of the elements needed to ensure survival.	Type 1: If comfortable, this type has no problem fitting in. However, this type does not take change too well especially stepping out of their comfort zone.	Type 1: A possessive and jealous nature is not uncommon for this type. Nevertheless, they can be counted on to be dependable partners.
Type 2: While they are caring and nurturing, they may feel entitled to having their needs met.	Type 2: Approval and recognition are important to this type. However, they do value positive relationships over position.	Type 2: They may become demanding in terms of attention. Yet, they can form deep and meaningful bonds with their significant other.
Type 3: This type is concerned with gaining material possessions which can ensure security. They have the drive and energy to accomplish significant results.	Type 3: They are all about knowing the right people and getting "in". They are genuine leaders and can take on responsibility as needed.	Type 3: They have powerful charisma. However, they may be unsure about the true power of their sexuality. They are very concerned about their self-image.
Type 4: They are willing to move on	Type 4: This type is constantly looking	Type 4: This type may show feelings

to new situations if needed. They may even make reckless decisions without thinking them through.	for the best possible social role. However, they may become envious of those who achieve what they cannot.	of inadequacy. They generally value themselves with the power and strength of others. As such, this comparison may lead to their valuation to rise and fall as a result.
Type 5: This type views their home as their castle. They might tend toward hoarding resources in case of an emergency.	Type 5: They are concerned with attaining symbols of social status. They may even find themselves in a position where they cannot fully interact with others due to their tendency to overthink things.	Type 5: This type tends to have very personal and deep relationships. However, they will demand space and autonomy even in most intimate relationships.
Type 6: This type's biggest security threat is the loss of connection with their family or social network. This need takes precedence over material ones.	Type 6: They will play a role as a protector or guardian in this community. Knowing where they stand in their community will go a long way toward helping them feel comfortable and secure.	Type 6: This type can overcome their fears by showcasing their courage. This will help demonstrate their ability to create stability and maintain control in their lives and relationships.

Type 7: This type is very much concerned about having an abundant lifestyle. They cannot bear the idea of waiting for something.	Type 7: It might seem contradictory, but this personality type is very much willing to sacrifice themselves for the good of their social group.	Type 7: They are carefree and spontaneous. New ideas and adventures are what keep them going. They can easily get by on charm.
Type 8: This type is built for survival in a dog-eat-dog world. They are not afraid to put up a fight to ensure survival.	Type 8: They will take on a leadership role in which they can set a common agenda that ensures everyone's wellbeing.	Type 8: This type can be very possessive and dominant. They are willing to let go if need be. However, they may have a hard time giving their partner enough space and room to breathe.
Type 9: These folks are collectors. They will gather as many resources as they can though they are not hoarders. They will use up resources as needed to ensure their comforts.	Type 9: These are selfless leaders who are devoted to the common good of the group. However, they may lose sight of the group's overall priorities.	Type 9: This type yearns to be at one with their partner. Thus, this may cause issues with boundaries at times. Therefore, it is important to make sure that there are clear rules in the relationship.

The subtypes which we have described above are the result of general guidelines. As such, the influence of wings, as well as the environment, needs to be taken into account. Nevertheless, they provide a very good rule of thumb to take into consideration.

Chapter 14

Triads

In this chapter, we are going to be looking at a component of the Enneagram known as the "triads". The triads are three intrinsic elements that negatively affect core personalities. What his means is that they are rooted in unhealthy patterns.

The Enneagram of Personality is comprised of a fundamental element known as the triads. As the name suggests, these are three components that make up a negative influence upon the core personality types. Consequently, these negative influences can lead each of the personality types into a pattern of behavior which may cause the individual to go down the path of disintegration as opposed to the path of integration.

Also, it is important to consider that a fundamental understanding of the way triads work can lead the individual to gain deeper insight into these negative influences and how they can go about offsetting such influences. Hence, understanding what the triads represent provides folks with the opportunity to fully comprehend the nature in which they can maintain a healthy and balanced outlook on life.

Here are the triads:

1. The first triad is known as "fear". This is the "thinking" triad as it is associated with more intellectual and mental processes.

2. The second triad is known as the "anger" triad. This is the "instinctual" triad and it is associated with unconscious feelings or "gut" feelings as they can be referred to.
3. The third triad is the "shame" triad. This is a purely emotional triad and its influence can be linked to emotional reactions from an individual.

Under this concept, all of the negative feelings that a person has can be boiled down to any one of the triads, or a combination of two, or all three. The triads all represent emotions, feelings, and thoughts that a person has about the role they play in their social group, their self-image and how they perceive the world around them. For example, if an individual feels threatened at work, that is, they fear losing their job, the root feeling is fear, though the causes of this fear may vary significantly.

ANGER

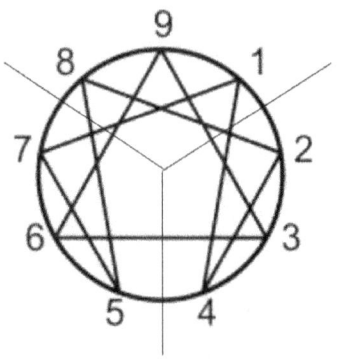

FEAR   SHAME

Adapted from: Fitzel.ca

As you can see in the image above, the triad cuts through the Enneagram in three equal parts. Therefore, anger is focused on 8, 9 and 1, shame on 2, 3 and 4 while fear is focused on 5, 6 and 7.

Besides, each one of these emotions has a specific action associated with it. For instance, anger is externalized, that is, it is projected outward. Likewise, shame is repressed or held in while fear and be internalized, that is, projected inward.

It is also important to note that each personality type hyper focuses on a specific part of the triad. What that means is that there is one specific emotion that tends to hit home more than the others. Here is what that looks like.

- Type 1: Internalizes anger.
- Type 2: Externalizes shame.
- Type 3: Represses shame.
- Type 4: Internalizes shame.
- Type 5: Externalizes fear.
- Type 6: Represses fear.
- Type 7: Internalizes fear.
- Type 8: Externalizes anger.
- Type 9: Represses anger.

Based on these reactions, you can cross-reference them to the core personality to see how that plays out in an individual's behavior. For example, Type Nine, the Peacemaker, will repress anger as much as possible. What that tells us is that a Type Nine, give the fact that they like to avoid conflict, will not express their anger outward. They will try to shove it way down to avoid an escalation in conflict.

Given this example, you can begin to link each one of these triads about the specific core personality. Now, it should be said that every core personality transitions through all of these emotions.

Yet, there is a specific hyper-focus on a single one of this triad. As such, you need to pay special attention to your core personality's hyper-focused emotion.

Consequently, let's take a look at some ways in which you can get a better grip on your hyper-focused emotions based on the triad.

- Type 1: This type tends to internalize anger, that is, focus in inward. Needless to say, this can become a dangerous and potentially self-destructive behavior as rather than lash out against other people or even the causes of their anger, they may lash out against themselves. As such, self-destructive behavior may lead to things such as addiction and substance abuse. That is why Type Ones need to find outlets for their feelings of anger, frustration and even guild.

- Type 2: This type tends to place shame outwardly, that is, on other folks. This can be seen by playing the "blame game". Consequently, Types Two need to avoid placing the blame on other people or making them feel bad when things don't go the way they expected. While taking responsibility for their actions is a great way to start, Type Twos should also focus on a collaborative effort in which placing responsibility squarely on one individual can be avoided.

- Type 3: This type's hyper-focus is to repress shame. What this means is that Type Threes will try to bury their feelings of guilt and inadequacy. While this may be effective for some time, these feelings will eventually come to the surface. When they do, they may leave the individual feeling emotionally distraught. This is why it is important to understand the source of these feelings and manage them accordingly. Often, counseling and having a support network can help alleviate these feelings before they even become an issue.

- Type 4: This type takes shame and focuses it on themselves. As such, they are prone to blaming themselves for the things that happen. This puts unnecessary pressure on themselves since not everything that happens in life is their fault. Of course, there is a need to take responsibility at times, but there is no need to bear the burden of everything that happens around them. Hence, it is important to be aware of these things which they can control and those which they cannot.

- Type 5: This type will project fear outward. This can come in the form of aggressive behavior. They may resort to intimidation and even certain levels of violence to get their way. That is why Type Fives need to avoid resorting to these tactics to get their way. It is often best to resort to dialogue to achieve a harmonious outcome.

- Type 6: This type is prone to swallow fear. Needless to say, this is not the healthiest of situations as shoving feelings way down only delays their ultimate effect. So, Type Sixes need to understand the source of their fears so that they can eventually face them and overcome them.

- Type 7: These types of projects fear inward. In the most extreme cases, this fear is enough to paralyze an individual and keep them from achieving anything in life. So, it is important to understand the root causes of fear and find adequate coping mechanisms for them. Often, having a support network is enough to help these types make their way through life.

- Type 8: This type tends to project their anger outward. Hence, the biggest challenge for this type is to exercise restraint and self-control. Naturally, uncontrolled outbursts can lead to irreparable consequences. Thus, exercising self-control becomes one of the most important things this type can do.

- Type 9: This type represses anger thereby become implosive. Over time, this implosive nature may lead to a serious emotional breakdown. Naturally, this is something that ought to be avoided at all costs. The main thing to keep in mind is that outlets are needed to vent pent up feelings. While there is no need for outbursts, there is the need for things such as exercise in which the individual can release the feelings they have been holding on to.

In general, a solid understanding of how the triads interact with your core personality will allow you to deal with these feelings more naturally. So, do take the time to go over the descriptions about how the triads affect your core personality and make a concerted effort to address these issues before they get the better of you.

Chapter 15

Determine Your Personality Type

In this chapter, we are going to be taking a deeper look at how you can go about determining your core personality type based on the model presented by the Enneagram of Personality.

Throughout this book, we have discussed the core personality types, the influence of wings and the triad. That is why further discussion is needed on how to determine your core personality type. In doing so, you will be able to establish your main characteristics and the influence that these have on the way you go about your life.

Now, it should be said that your core personality type is never expressed in pure form. In addition to the influence of your wings, there are environmental factors such as culture, socioeconomic status, religious beliefs and the circumstances that one must live through. All of these factors come into play when forging an individual's overall personality. Needless to say, there is no single factor that can perfectly mold a person's character.

Much like the Zodiac, the core personality type sets the foundation for a person's main traits though nothing is ever written in stone. When dealing with people, that is often the case. People are mutable and prone to change at any given moment especially when individuals make concerted efforts to improve upon or change aspects of their personality which they may wish to alter.

That being said, determine your personality type or that of those around you, is vitally important so that you can get the most out of the Enneagram model. At the outset of this book, we asked that you read through the descriptions of the nine personality types to get a feel for what they are like. Based on that, you could make an initial assessment as to which personality type fits in best with the way you perceive yourself.

Granted, that is not a foolproof method, but does allow you for an honest self-assessment. In doing so, it allows you to be honest with yourself and open the door for an exercise of introspection. Indeed, having the ability to be introspective enables you to become aware of the aspects which you feel you need to work on.

Naturally, there is a need for a more systematic and objective means of determining core personality types. As such, having a reliable means of testing is of the utmost importance. Of course, there are thousands of personality tests out there. There are some reputable and trustworthy tests such as the Myers-Biggs, which is essentially an industry standard, or less scientific tests like those found in the newspaper or the back of magazines.

Yet, all of these tests are ways in which you can find a more objective means of evaluating your personality type. This aims to take away any subjectivity that may come with making a personal assessment of one's personality.

In the case of the Enneagram, there are several types of tests out there. Earlier, we mentioned a couple of tests that are found on Enneagram websites. They are free and can be relied upon to provide you with a solid introduction to your core personality type.

Now, it should be pointed out that for most folks, a free test is enough to give them the spark they need to dig deeper into their personality. These free tests such as the one available at www.enneagramtest.com, can provide you with a great introduction into the nine core personality types. This test is a multiple-choice exam that you can do online. All you have to do is provide an email address in which your results will be sent to you. They do ask for donations after the results are provided, but that is entirely optional.

When you get your results, you will see a rather detailed description of that personality type. Once you have this core personality type, you can refer back to the Enneagram model and focus on your wings. So, if you are a Type One, then your wings will be 9 and 2. You would then need to look at their descriptions to gain a better sense of which of the wings is better suited to your personality.

As we mentioned in the section about wings, it is quite possible to influence both wings. While that is not entirely out of the question, it is more likely that you will have one predominant wing with a lesser influence from the other one. So, do take the time to go over both wings so that you can see where this influence might lie.

Another free option is the test offered by the Enneagram Academy. This test is a "light" version of the RHETI (more on that in a moment). This exam is much like the one offered by www.enneagramtest.com, and can be used to determine your core personality type. It consists of 36 multiple-choice questions. The results, while not scientifically validated, are rather accurate. So, it is certainly an option worth looking into.

John Turner

The industry standard in terms of Enneagram Personality testing is the RHETI or the Riso-Hudson Enneagram Type Indicator. This exam was developed by Don Riso and Russ Hudson in 2000. They devised a systematic method of testing personality types based on the Enneagram model. As such, they were able to develop a scientifically validated test that can accurately determine a person's core personality type.

The RHETI consists of 144 multiple-choice questions. It is generally offered as an online test through the Enneagram Institute (https://www.enneagraminstitute.com/). This organization is focused on providing training and testing services to individuals and companies.

The main difference between the RHETI and the other types of tests mentioned earlier is that the RHETI is a comprehensive evaluation whereas the other free test is an approximation to what your core personality type would. While the free examinations are still rather accurate, they are, by no means, guaranteed to be accurate. Thus, if you are looking for a reliable and scientifically validated means of determining your core personality type, then the RHETI is certainly an option.

According to the Enneagram Institute's website, the cost of taking the RHETI exam is $12 per access code. Each code can be used once. So, if multiple individuals wish to take the test, they would need to pay $12 per person. In exchange for that fee, a rather comprehensive evaluation is performed. Test takes receive quite a bit of information on that personality type and its potential influences. As such, it seems that the information provided is worth the fee that is paid for it.

Ultimately, it is highly recommended that you take at least one of these tests for you to determine your core personality type. The fact of the matter is that whether you choose the free or the paid version of the test, it is important to have an objective means of measuring your personality type. After all, these objective measures can help you establish your starting point.

The one limitation with the free tests is that they don't shed too much light into wings, triads, and levels of personal development in the same way that the full RHETI does. This is why free tests should be taken with a grain of salt. And while the full RHETI is by no means perfect, it is a far more accurate indicator of the full range of variables that play into the Enneagram core personality types.

If you would like to pursue further testing, taking a test such as the Myers-Biggs can also serve as another accurate measure in which you can compare and contrast the results of the RHETI. However, most corporations and private individuals for that matter have found the Enneagram to be a much simple and equally accurate measure.

Also, the RHETI tends to be a more cost-effective option insofar as the fee for the administering of the test is lower and takes a lot less time to perform as compared to a full-blown Myers-Biggs. Notwithstanding, if you, or your organization, have the time and can spare the cost, both tests would certainly be a worthwhile exercise.

One other important point to consider is that neither of these tests will give you an absolute, 100% description of your personality. As mentioned earlier, there is a myriad of factors that have molded and shaped your personality. Hence, it is important to account for these factors were reading through your core personality type.

So, it certainly pays to take a closer look into who you are, and how you got here. One very useful and valuable exercise, especially among family members and groups of co-workers, is to have a meeting to sit down and share results. By sharing results, everyone can get a better understanding of what drives on personality type, what their fears are, as well as, their negative and positive traits. This can lead to a deeper understanding of everyone in that group. At the end of the day, that is the main focus of this exercise: to improve relationships, both at a personal level, and a broader social level.

Chapter 16

The Enneagram and You

In this chapter, we are going to take a deeper look at the real-world applications of the Enneagram and how it can benefit you in the pursuit of your personal goals.

The main purpose of the Enneagram is to foster personal development. As seen in the lines of personal development, the Enneagram is designed to help you determine your starting point and where you can go from there. Even if you start at level 1 or level 9, there is always room for improvement. By the same token, there is always a chance that you could descend even further.

But barring those negative aspects, the Enneagram is meant to help you gain a better understanding of what makes you tick and what drives those around you. This is very important to keep in mind as understanding those around you is the best way to improve overall relationships. It can even help repair damaged or broken relationships since mutual understanding and acceptance are some of the keys to building healthy relationships.

Over time, your understanding of the core personality types will make it easier to deal with new folks. For example, part of the induction process of a new employee could be to take a simple, free Enneagram test. With the result, you can then better help the new co-worker become accustomed to their new surroundings.

When you see the results of this test you can say, "Oh, Mary is a Type Three". Then, you can better help Mary find her place in the company. Perhaps Mary thrives under pressure. Perhaps Mary chooses to avoid conflict. Or, perhaps Mary is a protector. Whatever the case, you can help Mary situate herself in a role, regardless of her actual job functions, that can help her make the best of her attributes.

This is why companies rely heavily on these types of tests. They use them to foster harmonious working relationships among employees and peers. This is a crucial element to consider especially when there are communication problems present in the workplace.

There have been many instances in which a company with communication issues decides to bring in a consultant to perform a test of this nature. Then, upon the results, co-workers are grouped into their core personality types. With this in mind, many folks come to the realization that they avoid responsibility, not because they are lazy or unmotivated, but because they are afraid of failure. So, the focus then shifts on how to better support this colleague as opposed to labeling them as lazy or uncooperative.

By the same token, there might be aggressive individuals in the company who lash out at others, not because they are mean or wish to harm others, but because that is the way they deal with their insecurities and issues. Often, this understanding is enough to diffuse a potential conflict in the workplace. Furthermore, it can help repair damaged relationships especially when significant conflict has taken place.

In other cases, more proactive and open leaders are willing to be transparent so that their subordinates can learn more about their boss' personality. This can help subordinates understand why a leader is permissive, demanding or even jealous. As such, this allows seeing where everyone is standing. In many ways, it's a means of playing on a level field.

On a personal level, the Enneagram is a great tool for self-discovery.

Many folks go through life wondering why they are the way they are, and why they feel the way they do. Often, this leads to large amounts of unnecessary stress. After all, not understanding why things are the way they are can be an enormous source of stress. Many people go through life trying to make sense of the things they do. Often, the answers don't come quite as easily as they would hope. This leads to further frustration and anguish.

As we saw in the levels of personal development, it is easy to fall into a trap of coping mechanisms. Everything from substance abuse, alcoholism, addiction to prescription medication and reliance on food can all lead to harmful coping mechanisms. Naturally, this does far more harm than good.

Nevertheless, when a person can make sense of their fears and their drivers, they can then begin to make far more progress based solely on their understanding of what drives them and what scares them. Indeed, gaining this understanding is a powerful force.

If you are reading this, as we speak, then you have already embarked upon a journey of self-discovery which will be hard to turn back on. By coming this far, you are acknowledging that there is far more to you than what meets the eye. Perhaps you have accepted the fact that there are aspects in your life which you wish to improve, but perhaps don't know where to begin.

Additionally, your road to self-discovery will take different paths. For instance, you may take a plunge before you can reemerge as a new person. Perhaps you might take a few dives before you can find peace and stability. We all go through it. But it is a lot worse when you have no idea why such things occur.

In this journey of self-discovery and self-improvement, it is important to keep your lines of integration and disintegration in clear sight.

We are constantly surrounded by circumstances that can, at one point or another, derail our efforts of making progress within our self-improvement. For instance, the loss of a loved one, an illness, or perhaps major setbacks such as losing a job or falling into financial distress can all derail any progress made toward finding a better emotional state. However, this is where your discovery will help you stay in tune with your feelings.

Let's consider this situation:

You are prone to using alcohol as a coping mechanism. While you are not an alcoholic, you tend to have a little too drunk to drink when you are feeling stressed out. Before gaining this knowledge, there wasn't much you could to do help it. But now that you do have this knowledge, you can identify the onset of such feelings. You are now capable of getting a better handle of the way you feel. Consequently, you can find a better way of handling your feelings as opposed to managing them with alcohol.

If you are the type that internalizes shame, you can better identify those feelings whenever they creep up. For example, if you are prone to blaming yourself for everything that happens, then you can take the time to ask yourself if everything that happens is your fault. You can ask yourself if you did everything you could have done to prevent the things that happened. Perhaps none of it was your fault yet you choose to blame yourself anyway.

By gaining greater insight into these feelings, you can avoid blaming yourself for everything that happens to you. Perhaps you are a victim in reality as opposed to the aggressor. By the same token, you can realize that the things that happen are your fault and you are responsible for them. Of course, this isn't about assigning blame. Quite the opposite, it is about being honest with yourself. At the end of the day, you don't need to show anything to anybody. There is nothing to prove. The only person whom you need, to be honest with is yourself. Others around you will feed off that honesty you have within yourself. Slowly, but surely, things will begin to fall into place.

At this point, you have everything you need to get started in the world of the Enneagram of Personality. You will find that the deeper you dig into it, the more fascinating it becomes. There is no denying that the insights that this model provides are extremely useful. While not 100% accurate, they are accurate enough to set you on a course in which you will find that your understanding of your personality, your motivators, and your fears will indeed set you free. Of course, changes do not occur overnight. However, the biggest step you can take is to open the door to self-discovery.

The ultimate goal of the Enneagram and this book for that matter is to get you on that road to self-discovery. As discussed with the lines of disintegration, one event can set you off the rails. But with the lines of integration, the opposite is true. Perhaps this book will be the catalyst that you have been looking for. Perhaps this message is what you need to get you back on track and the path to integration. Sure, it will not be easy. Yes, there will be some bumps along the way, but is that what makes this whole process fun?

Well, perhaps not fun, but certainly worthwhile. Please spare no efforts in improving yourself. There is always something which you can do to both improve yourself and achieve your goals. You can go about building yourself and your life one day at a time.

Conclusion

Thank you for reading this book. If you made it this far it is because you are truly interested in learning how the Enneagram of Personality can help you improve yourself and your relationships with those around you. Indeed, the Enneagram model can help you gain insights into yourself, and the people in your social group, that you might not have been able to achieve otherwise.

The fact of the matter is that the road to self-discovery is never easy. In fact, you may uncover some issues which may not be the most comfortable or the most pleasant. Yet, they are necessary to reveal. As has been stated before, there is nothing you need to prove to anyone but yourself. You only need to prove to yourself that you are committed to becoming the best possible version of yourself.

That can only happen when you are committed to making the most of the circumstances around you. If you don't feel like you have the knowledge you need, then the Enneagram model is the tool you need in order to get started.

What if you are experienced in your journey of self-discovery?

Then, the Enneagram will surely function as a very useful tool to complement the breakthroughs which you have already made. After all, nothing is perfect in this world. It is quite probable that this tool will help you uncover some deeper aspects of yourself that you might not have been aware of. Perhaps you might simply confirm aspects about yourself that you have been contemplating but perhaps couldn't quite place a finger on.

At this point, the next step to consider is taking the Enneagram personality test. You can begin with any one of the free tests which we have indicated herein. They are a great starting point in which you can determine your core personality. That is the foundation of the Enneagram. Without understanding your core personality, it will be quite hard for you to gain a strong foothold in your understanding of the Enneagram model.

As you progress through the discovery of your core personality, you may very well find aspects about yourself that you might not have previously thought were there. Perhaps you might be filled with Aha! moments.

The fact of the matter is that by starting off with a personality test, you can begin to place your feelings, ideas, reactions, motivators, and fears into a clearer context. These tests can help you to focus your attention on where it would be most useful.

Then, you can move onto more specific aspects such as the influence of your wings. Given the fact that wings are secondary influences into your main character, there is no doubt that studying them in greater detail will also provide you with the elements you need to get a much broader picture of who you are.

Naturally, the Enneagram will never paint a 100% accurate picture of who you are. There will be holes that need to be plugged. Those are more specific aspects which you can look into as you go through your life experience. For example, you fell off your bike as a child and broke your arm. This traumatic experience may explain why you don't like sports despite your personality type being very active. Perhaps your personality type is not prone to discipline, yet you had a very structured upbringing.

All of these aspects which are the product of your environment and your upbringing are all key elements that will help to round out the full picture of who you are. Hence, this is the reason why we say that the journey to self-discovery is not a short one.

If you feel compelled to dig even further into your Enneagram type, you can certainly look into taking the RHETI. The RHETI test is a great way in which you can get a very accurate picture of who you are, your levels of personal development, your wings and even your place in the triad. While the cost of this test is not prohibitive, you may choose to pay the fee or stick with the free versions out there.

Regardless of your choice, taking an Enneagram personality test is the best way in which you can get an objective assessment of your personality type. From there, you can share the information which you have learned with your friends, family, and co-workers. They will surely be interested in learning more about themselves and how to get along with those around them. Sure, there might be some folks who could care less. But the truth of the matter is, most people are always interested in learning more about themselves. Now, not everyone might be ready to face some of the unpleasantness that comes with self-discovery. Nevertheless, this could be the kickstart they need to get on the tracks of their lines of integration.

So, do take the time to share this message with anyone you feel would benefit from it. Perhaps you can all take the Enneagram personality test and embark on this journey of self-discovery as a unit. Often, having a buddy to urge you on is a great way of helping you keep your motivation high. Perhaps you can be the one to help others stay on the road to self-discovery and self-improvement. That is something which you can discover in your own personality type.

As always, please share your comments on this matter. Other readers, out there may be interested in this topic, yet they may not know where to start. As such, your comments will be valuable in helping them see the value in this book.

Hopefully, you have found the information in this book to be useful and insightful. So, please do share your ideas with others around you. They will surely be interested in knowing what you have to say on this topic. After all, there are no better recommendations than those that come from folks who have experience, firsthand, the value in this book.

If you enjoyed this book, please let me know your opinion by leaving a short review on Amazon. Thanks!